Samuel

The Inspiring Story of How an Amish Boy's Tragedy Brought Two Worlds Together

Robert J. Hastings

Based on the journals of
Oba and Lorene Herschberger

Published by
LONGSTREET PRESS, INC.
A subsidiary of Cox Newspapers,
A subsidiary of Cox Enterprises, Inc.
2140 Newmarket Parkway
Suite 122
Marietta, GA 30067

Printed in the United States of America

1st Longstreet printing, 1997

Library of Congress Card Catalog Number 97-71926

ISBN: 1-56352-437-6

Book design by Laura McDonald
Cover design by Audrey Graham
Cover photography by Bill Foley / UNIPHOTO
Electronic film prep by OGI, Forest Park, GA

Back cover artwork illustrated by Samuel J. Butcher

Contents

Foreword

In the summer of 1864, Joel Beachy of Maryland and Moses Yoder of Pennsylvania came West, looking for fertile land for Amish settlers. During a Sunday stopover in Pana, Illinois, they took a walk in the country as far as Neoga. They liked what they saw. Monday morning, they took a train to Mattoon, then walked fourteen miles to Arcola. Here they spent a day or so, looking at more farmland.

They returned in September to negotiate for land. Others followed them, and today their Old Order Amish descendants, some 650 families, live in a twenty-two square-mile area from Sullivan to Tuscola, Arthur being about the center.

The Amish trace their roots to the Mennonites and Anabaptists who flourished in Germany and Switzerland during the Protestant Reformation in the 1500s. Cruelly persecuted in Europe because of their antimilitary beliefs, the Mennonites and Amish began emigrating to the United States in large numbers in 1740.

Although they have common roots with the Mennonites, the Amish tend to be more conservative in dress, living habits, and doctrine. The most conservative are known as the "Old Order Amish." Although they pay income taxes and affirm loyalty to the government, the Old Order Amish do not serve in the military, do not accept government farm subsidies, do not vote in state and national elections, and do not own automobiles, televisions, radios, or buy electricity.

They do not buy life or health insurance, nor do they

insure their homes and farm buildings, depending instead on self-insurance programs through their churches. They worship in homes and choose their nonsalaried, bivocational ministers for life. Amish children are baptized at an age when they can decide for themselves, normally between the ages of sixteen and twenty. Formal education ends at the eighth grade. Family-centered, they reject divorce and care for their elderly in their own homes. They often describe themselves as the "Quiet People."

One of the Illinois Old Order Amish families is the Oba Herschbergers, who live five miles southeast of Sullivan. Early on the morning of August 22, 1991, one of the family's thirteen children, Samuel, then nine years old, was tragically injured in a farm accident.

For weeks, he clung to life at the Memorial Medical Center in Springfield. One doctor noted, "Hurt like that, he shouldn't be here; there must be a God." Samuel's parents stayed with him in the hospital, day and night, for eight weeks. Dressed in Amish clothing, they soon became a familiar sight.

Due in part to a series of articles written by Judy Miller for the *State Journal-Register* and widely distributed by the Associated Press, thousands of readers were caught up in Samuel's struggle to live, as well as in the plight of his parents, who, like most Amish, had no health insurance.

Samuel returned to the hospital many times, largely for reconstructive surgery. A variety of benefits in central Illinois helped with his expenses.

When I learned that his parents, Oba and Lorene, might want to write about their experiences, I volunteered my services to help them put the story together. They gladly accepted, resulting in a rewarding friendship. My wife and I have been to their farm, and they've visited us. We introduced them to Chinese food, and they invited us to the wedding of their son David.

Fortunately, Lorene kept a 409-page journal, and Oba had made notes from time to time. I read these carefully, intent on the feelings they conveyed as much as the facts.

I interviewed Lorene and Oba several times, reviewing the details of their traumatic experiences. I also assembled a file of Judy Miller's articles and Samuel's medical records. Also, I interviewed many of the doctors, chaplains, nurses, paramedics, friends, and relatives mentioned herein.

With this information, I proceeded like working a jigsaw puzzle, to piece their story together. What you will read are not always their exact words, but are their exact feelings. Nor is this book a reprint of their journals. While the journals provided the broad outline, many, many details were gleaned from newspaper clippings and interviews.

The reader will note that at times, the tense jumps from the past to the present, then back again. This is intentional; it is not an error in editing. Persons under stress often change tenses in their conversations, and such changes are reflected in the journal entries. I chose to preserve this flavor and style in the completed manuscript.

Since Oba and Lorene did not get to meet all of the people who befriended Samuel, there's no way to include everyone who played a role.

I'm depositing copies of their original journals, my interview notes, related correspondence, and newspaper clippings with the Illinois State Historical Library in Springfield, where interested readers, with certain restrictions, may further pursue the story.

Special thanks to Samuel J. Butcher for permission to reprint on the cover his sketch of an Amish boy. To Raymond Bial for permission to use the photographs on the cover. To Mary Ellen McElligott for her superior editing skills. To Mark A. Ritterbusch and Theresa Lascody for excellence in typography and design of the original book. To the Helen Steiner Rice Foundation of Cincinnati, OH, for permission to reprint "People Need Friends." To Stephanie Markou George at Memorial Medical Center and Susan Helm of the Southern Illinois University School of Medicine for scheduling interviews with medical personnel. To the Memorial Medical Center for the use of their boardroom for a week of interviews.

To my dentist, Peter E. Glatz, DDS, for introducing me, in his Spring, 1996 newsletter, to a timely quote by Will Durant, author of *The Story of Civilization.* Although, in his lifetime, Dr. Durant never knew the Oba Herschberger family, he surely had this kind of people in mind when he wrote:

> *Civilization is a stream with banks. The stream is sometimes filled with blood from people killing, stealing, shouting and doing things historians usually record, while on the banks, unnoticed, people build homes, make love, raise children, sing songs, write poetry. The story of civilization is what happened on the banks. Historians are pessimists because they ignore the banks for the river.*

And finally, to my wife, Bessie, who never lost faith this book would somehow, some way, be published.

Robert J. Hastings
Springfield, Illinois

Names and ages
Oba and Lorene Herschberger family,
August 22, 1991

Oba	42
Lorene	41
Paul	21
Paul's wife, Rosanna	21
Paul's baby, Marneta	3 weeks
Chris	20
Duane	19
Susanna.	17
David	16
Joseph	14
Steven	13
Rosanna	11
SAMUEL	9
William	8
John	7
Philip	5
Mary Anna	3

As of this date, Oba's parents, Chris and Amelia Herschberger of rural Arthur, had 401 direct descendants. Lorene's parents, Chris and Lizzie Bontrager, were deceased; their descendants also number in the hundreds.

A Father's Premonition

Do you believe in premonitions — those nagging, half insights about the future? A quiet premonition wormed its way into my mind on Wednesday, August 21, 1991, the day before my son Samuel's brush with death. I remember it well — too well.

"Breakfast's on!" cried my wife Lorene from inside our farm home, five miles southeast of Sullivan, Illinois. The aroma of bacon and eggs filled the morning air. We'd been up since five o'clock, doing the morning chores and milking our thirty-two Holstein cows.

With work-honed appetites, we quickly settled into fourteen chairs around our long kitchen table — Lorene and I, plus twelve of our thirteen children. In Amish tradition, we bowed our heads in silent prayer. After eating, we had our morning devotions. Little did I know that would be our last normal breakfast for many weeks.

Once the table was cleared, Lorene told Susanna, seventeen, and Rosanna, eleven, to pick some green beans from our half-acre garden for dinner and to watch after Mary Anna, almost four, and Philip, five. "It may be 12:30 before Oba and I get home, so don't start the beans too soon," she added.

I told the older boys, aged seven to twenty, to fill the silo while we were gone. It was corn harvest time, and the green silage needed to be chopped for cattle feed. I warned them to be careful, knowing there's always danger on a farm, especially around the chopper and blower.

I hitched up one of our buggies for the five-and-a-half-mile drive to the Jonathan Creek School, one of twelve parochial schools in our area for Amish children. (Jonathan Creek Church is also the name of our congregation.) Lorene and I were on the school board, and this was clean-up day before the fall opening on Friday. Since five of our children would be pupils (including Samuel, starting fourth grade), we took special interest.

As we started out of the yard, Samuel, nine, came running out of the house wearing a big grin and a new straw hat; his blond hair, freshly cut for school, peeked from under the wide brim. "*Kann ich mit geh?*" (Can I go with you?) he asked impishly.

"Sure," I said, scooting over to make room between me and Lorene. "But why did you decide to go?"

"Oh, I just thought I should."

Lorene and I exchanged puzzled looks, for Samuel was a stay-at-home boy. Going anywhere was a treat for his nine brothers — wherever I go, there's always a boy tagging along — but not for Samuel. Right then came the premonition. Lorene sensed it too, she told me later.

This feeling was a strange and unwelcome guest to our inseparable family, which — like all Amish families — is closely knit and lives near to the soil. Whereas many English people (our term for the non-Amish) delight in television, radio, air conditioning, cars, tractors, boom boxes, movies, and telephones, we find joy in the traditional patterns of farm life dating back generations to our Swiss and German ancestors.

The rhythm and flow of planting and harvesting; birthing

our children; erecting our own homes and barns; reveling in camping, fishing, hunting, and ice skating; family dinners and festive weddings; caring for our sick and aged — these offer their own rewards. We feel rich, indeed.

We moved to our farm east of Sullivan in 1988, buying ninety-two acres and renting fifty more. We enjoy the rolling terrain of hills and wooded groves, in contrast with the open flatlands near Arthur and Tuscola, Illinois, where we grew up.

True, our 108-year-old farmhouse was nothing to brag about. But with free labor from a big family of boys and help from relatives, we knew we could add on to the house and outbuildings later, so we put our initial money into land.

Our house (I once called it a "shack"), had three small bedrooms, a tiny kitchen, a living room, one bath, and a cellar that flooded each spring. We heated with a wood-burning stove in the living room. When we moved here, seven of the boys slept in one room — four in bunk beds and three on pallets between the beds. The three girls had their own room, and the other three boys slept on bunk beds in my and Lorene's room. By 1991, however, we had moved a three-room trailer into our backyard, where six of the boys slept.

As our buggy pulled out on the main road, headed north to the school, I noticed Boots, our Australian Blue Heeler, standing near the house with a pitiful look — a look he assumed whenever any of us started to leave. Boots was the smartest dog I ever had, so smart he could almost read my mind. He was a no-nonsense work dog who gloried in rounding up the livestock.

Driving through the countryside, lost in the beauty of an August morning, we forgot our apprehension. To me, a buggy ride along a country road is one of the most relaxing joys of our Amish culture. I guess it's the rhythmic clatter of horses' hooves, the broad, late-summer fields of corn and oats, the big sky overhead, a rabbit scurrying across the road, a circling hawk looking for dinner, a wash hanging on the line, a breeze in your face, a dog barking in the distance, a friendly neighbor waving as you pass — all of which are serene and reassuring to me.

We talked about our joy over the birth of our first grandchild, Marneta, born just three weeks earlier to our son Paul and his wife, the former Rosanna Otto. Holding Marneta for the first time, I said, "Look, I'm too young to be a grandpa!" Marneta brought a new seriousness to my life, more so even than the birth of my own children. It was as if this grandchild was a tangible link to our heritage, to our past, present, and future.

As we neared the school, Samuel asked if he could work, and I said he could help mow. "Good deal!" he cried in English, not knowing the German equivalent. He jumped from the buggy before we even stopped. Lorene and I joined about a dozen other volunteers.

Since we Amish accept no federal or state tax monies, each family pays $800 to $1,200 tuition a year, plus donated labor for upkeep of the school and property. While the women cleaned the inside from top to bottom, the men did some painting and repairs to the building, which includes two classrooms, a full basement, indoor toilets, and a small barn to house the pupils' horses during school hours.

Meanwhile, Samuel helped mow the big playground and ball diamond.

"Anything else?" he asked, as I was painting a swing.

"No, that's all for today." But for a brief moment, my uneasiness returned — an anxiety I couldn't define or explain.

We arrived home about one o'clock for a late dinner. Since the chopper had broken down, the older boys had left the silo unfilled. I told them we'd get it fixed and finish the task tomorrow.

That afternoon, a horse trader stopped by to show me one of the finest standard-bred mares I'd ever seen. I keep about twenty-five horses all the time, which I sell as well as use for our field work. Belgians are my favorite breed for hard, steady work. For our buggies, however, we use standard-bred mares, a popular breed for sulkies racing. They make excellent buggy horses.

We haggled over the price a bit, for he was asking more than I could afford. But she was top quality, and I really wanted her. We finally agreed on a price. Her name was Ann, and she was the finest mare I had ever owned.

When I stabled her for the night, I had no idea I'd never see her again. Nor that I'd never whistle to Boots again as he scurried across the pasture. Unknown to us, a gathering storm was headed our way, a storm that would forever change Samuel and every other member of our family.

Part 1: The Storm

(Oba and Lorene as separate voices)

1. A Tragedy at Sunrise

THURSDAY, AUGUST 22, 1991

Oba: The sun was peeking over the horizon as we headed for the barn to milk our Holsteins. The cows saw our familiar faces, and a series of *moo-moo*s rippled down the long line of stalls. "Come on, Bossy, time to be milked," I called, while Lorene readied the automatic milkers and our older boys began feeding the sows and horses at the other end of the barn.

Samuel asked if David, sixteen, could pull a wagon full of feed into the barn so the horses could eat directly from the wagonbed. "I can unhitch the wagon while David stays on the tractor," Samuel said. I agreed, warning him — as I routinely did all the boys — to be careful. He set out in a full tilt to catch up with David.

Some minutes later, when we were about half done with the milking, David came tearing in the barn, breathless. "Mom! Dad!" he shouted. "Come quick! I think Samuel's dead!"

I dropped the milkers and raced out of the barn. As I ran the hundred yards to the feeding lot, the thought of yesterday's chilling premonition flashed through my mind.

I was there first, and what I saw will haunt me as long as I live. Stripped practically naked and bloodied, our precious, blond-headed Samuel — three days from his tenth birthday — was wrapped around the PTO (power take off) of the tractor like a corkscrew.

The PTO is a steel shaft about four feet long and two inches square. When attached to the rear drive of a tractor, it can spin at hundreds of revolutions per minute to transfer power to other machines. As Samuel released the hitch pin to unhook the PTO from the tractor, in preparation for hitching the wagon, the PTO had started spinning wildly. It shouldn't have, but it did. And it should have been covered by a safety shield, but it wasn't; I had removed the shield several days earlier to work on the PTO.

The whirling shaft had snagged Samuel's clothes and snatched him out of his shoes, instantaneously turning his body into a small, twisted ball of flesh. His shredded clothing was wrapped around his body like a cocoon, binding him to the shaft. His head was scalped, the hair and flesh almost ripped off. His right arm was grotesquely twisted around the left side of his head, the cold, steel shaft locking his hand to his cheek. His left arm hung by a sliver of flesh from his shoulder. His right leg was almost severed in two places. Broken bones protruded from his left leg.

No experience prepares a man for such a sight, especially of his child. With my heart pounding in my chest, I turned away from the grisly scene, thinking Samuel dead.

Just then I heard a tiny voice whisper, "Dad . . . please . . . *grick mich do raus*!" ("get me out of here.")

I gasped and turned around. Samuel had opened his eyes! I don't remember if I answered his plea or not. But I knew I was helpless to free his twisted body, so I ran to the home of a non-Amish neighbor to telephone for emergency help. When I got there, I found my son Duane, who had already called for help.

By now a deadly fear was twisting itself around my heart, just as Samuel was twisted around the PTO. Adding to my terror was a sudden surge of guilt, because I knew I had put off replacing the safety shield on the PTO.

Lorene: I reached Samuel just as Oba left to get help. Never had I seen such horror! Trembling with fear, I knelt beside

Samuel and reached under him to support his lower body. When he tried to lift his legs, I could see they were badly broken. I wanted to turn and run away but couldn't. I had to stay. My heart was breaking.

I wanted to keep him conscious, fearing that if he slipped away he might not return. Then just as suddenly as my fear and trembling had come, they faded away. I felt the Lord's unmistakable presence.

I reached up and pushed the torn scalp back in place as best I could. Oh, Lord, how can he be alive? With chattering teeth little Samuel asked, "Mom, will I die?" I said I hoped not, and we prayed. Oh, my poor, poor boy.

He never cried or lost consciousness. I told him when I heard the ambulance coming and when I saw it pulling in the drive. He said he was cold; I told him the medics would have a blanket, which they did.

Quietly, so that Samuel couldn't hear, I told Susanna and Rosanna to stay back. I didn't want them to see this.

The paramedics from the Sullivan Rescue Squad started an IV into one arm, but since it was almost severed, the liquid spilled out onto the ground. With a big, surgical-like knife, they cut away what was left of the shredded pants and shirt that bound Samuel to the shaft. I asked one of the paramedics if I should get out of the way, but he said, "No, Mom, just keep talking to him." So I talked to him in English, then German, making sure he heard me: "Keep your eyes open, Samuel. Don't go to sleep; you'll be okay."

Thinking I could take no more but knowing that I had to, I forced myself to hold him close while they unraveled his body from around the shaft.

The paramedics secured Samuel to a spineboard and loaded him into the ambulance. I took off my chore apron, and a neighbor handed me my purse, bonnet, and crochet bag that I'd sent to the house for. Someone took hold of me and said, "This way, Mom," and put me in the front seat of the ambulance.

I wish I'd turned around and comforted the children, told them not to be afraid and to practice their faith, that things will work out, but I didn't. It was all so fast.

Samuel never lost consciousness and bled very little. One of the nurses said she thought his body was twisted with such force that the exposed blood vessels were virtually clamped, allowing them to clot quickly. I can't bear to think about it, but the PTO evidently yanked him so hard that he was literally jerked out of his shoes, for they were left in the same position as when it happened.

The nurse, Gina, also was having a hard time keeping calm. She asked Samuel if he was doing all right. "Yes," he whispered, "but if I die it's okay. And if I live it's okay."

Oba: Our yard was filled with neighbors who heard the sirens. At the accident scene, my legs refused to move. Lorene was comforting Samuel, and the paramedics were working to free him. Someone took my arm and reassured me there was nothing I could do. Not wishing to just stand there, I ran back to the barn where the smaller children waited, terrified. I told them to stay calm, to finish their chores, that Mom and I were going with the ambulance. Two of our non-Amish neighbors, Richard and Julie Day, said they would drive me to the hospital while Lorene rode in the ambulance.

While we waited for them to load Samuel, one of the sightseers standing in the yard said to me, "Oba, you know this is your fault." I felt the blood rush out of my face and my chest tighten as if it were being squeezed by a giant hand. How could anyone say that at a time like this? Especially when I was already blaming myself. How could I bear this guilt?

All the way to the hospital I kept asking myself, "Why

did I let Samuel help with the feeding? Why hadn't I replaced the PTO shield?"

Lorene: When they unloaded Samuel at St. Mary's Hospital, I leaned against the ambulance, thinking I might faint. A nurse took my arm and asked me to follow her, which I did with leaden feet. There was Samuel on a stretcher, and all I could see was part of his face. He looked at me, saying softly, "It hurts." His lips quivered so fast I could barely understand him.

A doctor came and told us they needed to send Samuel to Memorial Medical Center, a major trauma center in Springfield, about forty miles away. They hurriedly made some X rays to send along, gave him a tetanus booster, and inserted a catheter, which made him cry. I wanted to tell them, "Don't do that now! He's got enough pain!"

They called for a helicopter, but none was available, so Samuel would have to be driven in an ambulance. They had little hope he would survive until we reached Springfield. One of the medics, a thirty-year veteran, said he'd never known anyone to live, cut up like that. Then Julie and Richard Day, friends who had driven Oba to the hospital, walked in. I just held Julie tight, and for the first time I let myself cry.

Oba: Richard and another non-Amish neighbor, Novie Waddell, sat in the waiting room with us. Unbeknownst to me, these two men hadn't spoken to each other for a long time, due to some little misunderstanding. I still don't know what it was.

Anyway, as we waited, Novie got up and walked over to Richard and, with tears in his eyes, asked, "Will you forgive me for the way I've acted toward you?"

Richard said "Yes," and that he was sorry too, and they shook hands. Truly, the Lord works in mysterious ways "his wonders to perform." A very appropriate Bible verse came to me: "And a little child shall lead them."

Lorene: Novie drove me and Oba to Springfield, following the ambulance. I sat in the back seat. Never has a forty-mile trip seemed so long. The minutes crept by. I wanted to tell Novie to drive faster, to keep up with the ambulance, but knowing they would start work on Samuel whether we were there or not, I was consoled.

Oba: The midmorning sun was so pretty when we arrived at Memorial Medical Center — bright and clear. How could this nightmare be happening on such an otherwise glorious day? But it was.

Looking for directions, we saw a sign to the emergency entrance and a friendly woman's face motioning us on. Inside, she gave us a hug. "We'll help you through this," she promised. Her name was Veronica — Chaplain Veronica Higgins, a Catholic nun. She took us into a private room and asked if we would like to pray.

Lorene: Veronica was like an angel. First she offered us something to drink. Then we knelt — the four of us, including Novie, our driver. Three faiths, kneeling together, holding hands, praying to the same God in Heaven. I'd never prayed with a Catholic, nor with Novie, a member of the Mt. Zion Baptist Church near Sullivan.

While we prayed, doctors in the adjoining trauma room were doing CAT scans and X rays of Samuel. Four of them soon came to see us. They showed us they cared. They knelt by our chairs and in low, whispered tones, explained the seriousness of his condition. They could make no promises, but Samuel remained conscious and answered their questions.

As they filed out, Oba and I wept uncontrollably. Sister

Veronica cried too. Then a nurse came and said we could see Samuel before he went to surgery.

Oba: We could hardly believe what we saw. Samuel's injuries were so messy and gory that there was no place to touch him or even hold his hand. He was in shock, his blood pressure dangerously low. One doctor said he should have bled to death, that there was no reason why he was alive — that God must be with him. He'd never known a patient to survive such injuries.

Samuel's teeth were chattering, and he begged for water. Just a simple drink, but we couldn't give him one — only a wet washcloth on his lips. He asked if, like his brother Joseph who had suffered a broken bone earlier, he had to wait before they set his broken bones — as if those were the worst of his injuries.

We said good-bye for now and told him to ask Jesus to be with him. He nodded his head. It was noon when he entered surgery. With heavy hearts, we left him.

As the afternoon wore on, they moved us to a waiting room near Surgery and promised a report every two hours. Janet Hatmaker, another Catholic chaplain, sat with us awhile and prayed. One of her sons was fourteen. She seemed to sense the pain that parents feel when their children suffer.

Lorene: Friends came to share our vigil — our son Paul and his wife, Rosanna; Oba's sister Mary and his brother Monroe and his wife; also William Otto, the bishop of our church; Levi Otto, a deacon; and the Ivan Schrocks.

Realizing that we hadn't eaten all day, Novie and Oba went for food about 8:00 p.m., but we couldn't get anything down. Finally they threw the food away.

Shortly afterward a doctor came and told us they were ready to reattach Samuel's left arm and that they would have to shorten his right leg four inches, due to damage to the bones and cartilage. It was midnight and he had been in surgery nearly twelve hours. All were gone home except Mary. Everything was so quiet, like death.

Oba: A night cleaning woman stopped to ask if we needed anything. Her concern, even though she didn't know us, touched me. She first brought us a bag of ice for drinks, then some blankets. Although we were already well supplied, there was something about her motherly concern that helped to shorten the night. We'll never forget her.

FRIDAY, AUGUST 23, 1991

Lorene: At 4:00 a.m. a nurse told us that the doctors hadn't even stopped to eat. Some students from Southern Illinois University School of Medicine were observing, she said. The doctors were ready to reattach Samuel's scalp, but because it had been nearly twenty-four hours since the accident, they were concerned that it wouldn't take.

A little later Dr. David Olysav told us all of Samuel's fractures were set but that there was bleeding in his lungs, which sent our hopes spiraling downward. He had been given thirteen units of blood. He had no major head or spinal injuries, and that was a plus for him.

At 6:00 a.m., after eighteen hours in surgery, Samuel was taken to the recovery room, but it would be hours before we could see him. They told us we should try to eat something, but in the cafeteria the food again stuck in our throats; Oba and I just looked at each other and shook our heads. Instead of eating, we went to the hospital chapel where it was quiet, to meditate.

We were only seventy miles from the farm, but home seemed so far away, and Oba continued to blame himself for the accident.

Finally, at 3:30 p.m., they said, "You can see Samuel now." We were glad but dreaded how he might look.

Oba: When we walked into Samuel's room, it looked like his chance of survival was zero. One leg and both arms were in casts, suspended in midair. One leg, heavily bandaged, lay supine on the bed. Thick dressings covered his back. His head was wrapped in gauze, and his face so swollen he looked like a grown, husky man. Both eyes were swollen shut, one blackened. Bruises covered his torso. But oddly, there were no cuts on his face. He was connected to various devices and IVs, plus a ventilator to help him breathe and a tube to drain the blood from his lungs. He was restless — constantly lifting his head and banging it down on his pillow.

But our Saviour is the Great Physician.

That night, all twelve of our other children, plus Paul's wife and new baby, came in a van to visit. We let them see Samuel two at a time, warning them not to be shocked. One of them said, "But it doesn't look like Samuel." And he didn't. Nothing looked as it should. Our whole world was turned upside down and inside out.

When Paul came back to the waiting room, he said, "Dad, we'll lose the farm ... everything!" Paul had always been work-oriented, very practical. I had been so worried about Samuel that I had given no thought to costs. The Amish don't believe in health insurance. In emergencies, we help each other. But in such an extreme case as this, I guess we could lose the farm. Where would we live, with twelve children still at home? A new worry crept into my mind.

Lorene: Before the children went home, we asked the nurses if we could sing for Samuel. Although he was unconscious, we thought maybe he could hear our singing. The nurses said to go ahead, so we joined hands and sang:

Jesus loves me, this I know,
For the Bible tells me so;
Little ones to Him belong,
They are weak but He is strong.

That was our only way to tell Samuel we were there, and that we all loved him. Maybe it wasn't proper, because hospitals must have rules. But the ICU charge nurse told us that we could do whatever cheered him up. And she said we could never know what our singing meant to the nurses, too. May God have all the glory.

2. One Hour, One Step, One Day

SATURDAY, AUGUST 24, 1991

Oba: We arrived here Thursday in our work clothes with traces of barn manure still on our shoes, but with no money, no wallet, no nothing. The hospital gave us vouchers for the cafeteria, and last night the children brought us clean clothes. We learned that we can shower on the second floor. As long as they'll let us, we have no intention of leaving Samuel, day or night.

Lorene: Two more hours of patchwork surgery for Samuel today, changing dressings and so forth. They put him on a special Kinair bed with an air mattress. A small fan circulates warm or cool air to different parts of the mattress. This prevents bed sores and also warms or cools Samuel as needed. I asked about the ventilator, and they said it helped Samuel breathe easier. While he is sedated with so much morphine, his body tends to relax and he doesn't breathe deeply enough to circulate blood to his brain and other tissues. The ventilator makes up for this.

They also started a nutrition drip — liquid fluids direct to his stomach through a plastic tube in his nose. While on the ventilator he can't talk, so they provided a plastic booklet with pictures and words he can point to, such as Mom or Bathroom. But he's too sick to use it.

I apologized to a nurse for asking so many questions, but we Amish always care for our own, and I want to know all I can. If Samuel lives to go home, then I can take better care of him.

We had lots of visitors today from Sullivan and Arthur. People here must think we Amish are taking over the hospital. We do stand out, the women with our long dresses and bonnets, and the men with beards and wide-brimmed hats. Levi and Edna Herschberger will stay with us tonight. There's nothing they can do, but just knowing they're here gives us comfort.

Oba: My thoughts kept turning to home — the chores, the fall harvest, the canning and freezing for winter, the milking, and the children starting school. There's so much farm work this time of year, and here we were in Springfield. But I told myself to be calm; God will see us through.

Last night, Larry and Donna Neuman of nearby Chatham were here. Although not Amish, they know many of our people, and any time the Amish are hospitalized in Springfield, the Neumans want to help. It's interesting how Larry got to know us. As a farmer himself, he admired our simple approach to life. In the fall of 1985, while driving through the Arthur area, they stopped at the home of David D. and Lizzie Schrock. David, who's also a minister, had a "Potatoes for Sale" sign out front. The Neumans were so impressed with David's explanation of how faith in Christ is our only basis for salvation that they later attended some of our services, plus a wedding or two. They're active in Parkway Christian Church in Springfield but good friends to all Amish.

We had a new nurse tonight. She seemed nervous and slow with the morphine. Watching Samuel suffer, I grew impatient and talked to the charge nurse. She told me to relax, that Samuel was in such poor condition they didn't want to hurry and make a mistake. Later, the new nurse put her arms around Lorene and apologized: "I have a ten-year-old at home, and when I look at Samuel, I see my own son." Then the three of us wept together.

SUNDAY, AUGUST 25, 1991

Lorene: Today was Samuel's tenth birthday. I woke at 4:00 a.m. and went in to see him. He was hot with fever, couldn't talk but motioned that his head hurt. The nurses brought a cake and taped a "Happy Birthday" streamer to his TV screen. Della Holdman, the cleaning woman, brought balloons and caramel corn. Samuel couldn't eat and we weren't sure he was conscious, but tears formed in his swollen eyes when Oba and I sang "Happy Birthday."

All the children came in the afternoon. I'm glad Samuel looked better, as they were shocked at his condition Friday night.

MONDAY, AUGUST 26, 1991

Oba: Once a day we visit the Bunn Chapel, just off the main foyer of the hospital, to pray. This morning my brother Eli gave a short talk. He said to live one hour at a time and to trust God for help as we need it. Maybe down the road we can look back and see this nightmare as a blessing. I don't know. There's a peace in suffering that's hard to explain. The Bible says through many tears we reach heaven.

Although we Amish worship in homes rather than in church buildings, I enjoy the quiet and beauty of the chapel.

Someone told us we should stop praying for Samuel so he could die in peace, free from suffering. The truth is, we've never demanded anything of God. Our wish has always been, "Thy will be done." Samuel is in His hands.

Yes, we pray. But God is in control, not us.

We know that back home our congregation, the Jonathan Creek Church, is praying for us. Jonathan Creek is one of twenty-three churches in the roughly twenty-two square miles of Amish country stretching from Sullivan to Tuscola. Each church has about thirty member families.

We meet in homes every other Sunday. Other Sundays are for visiting the sick and spending time with family and friends. A service, in German, lasts about two and a half hours. Each church has two ministers, one deacon, and one bishop. These men are chosen by lot and serve for life. They receive no salary. Both ministers prepare for Sunday, then we select one by lot to preach.

The men and boys sit separately from the women and girls. Although we sing hymns, we use no instruments, such as an organ or piano. We sit on benches with no backs, which we haul from house to house in a specially designed bench wagon. I long for a return to that normalcy.

Lorene: Samuel has had thirty-one units of blood so far. He went back to surgery for new dressings and to check on drainage from his scalp. His right foot was warm, and the pulse there was strong. They also grafted some skin from his arm pit to cover an exposed vessel on his arm. There's one circle of exposed flesh on his left arm where there's no skin at all.

Dr. Russell was encouraging about Samuel's right leg, now four inches shorter than his left one. There's a new technique for lengthening bones, called the "Ilizarov Fixator." This will come later, but his explanation gives us hope. It's nice of him to explain in language we understand.

Oba: Four of our children started school today. Classes began Friday, but they were too upset to go. They go in our two-seater open buggy. I hope they remembered all their books and lunches and drove carefully. Early mornings, some motorists get in a hurry, impatient of slow-moving buggies. All we can do is turn them over to God.

Lots of phone calls today — fifteen when we went down to lunch. We never tire of hearing from friends. Some families post "No visitors" signs. I'm sure they have their reasons, but we'd never keep anyone out. Samuel needs people; we need people; we'll never make it alone. Our visitors always bring box lunches and treats; these nourish our souls as well as our bodies.

I left Lorene with Samuel to go buy some stamps. While I was gone, Lorene couldn't hold back the tears, watching Samuel suffer. He suddenly opened his eyes a little and said, "Don't worry, Mom. God can heal me."

Today the Sullivan paper printed a story about the accident. I guess I was naive, but when a reporter called, I thought she was merely concerned. The Amish avoid publicity. We don't want our pictures in print. I fear our neighbors will think we put the story in ourselves. I regret I talked to the reporter.

Tonight was rough. Samuel wanted me to read to him. I showed him several children's books, but he shook his head no. Then I picked up a Bible storybook, and he nodded yes. I read until he fell asleep.

TUESDAY, AUGUST 27, 1991

Oba: Paul and Rosanna, with month-old Marneta, moved home today to take care of our children. They had been staying just nights, but Paul quit his job at Plank's Buggy Shop to work full-time on both farms, his and ours. They live a mile west of us on a fourteen-acre hog farm. He'll check on his feeder pigs twice a day, while looking after our thirty-two Holsteins, two hundred chickens, two hundred feeder pigs, and my band of mares. Plus the fall harvest. Rosanna will help with the cooking, laundry, canning, and sewing. There will be fourteen of them altogether — quite a responsibility for a new mother, herself only twenty-one.

Lorene: Samuel developed a new problem today — a yeast infection. An infection specialist told us the yeast infection is a fungus that antibiotics can't control. Worse still, the strong antibiotics they have been giving Samuel have also weakened his resistance to the fungus.

Oba: This yeast infection is terrible. It's on his abdomen and genitals. Before I learned to wear rubber gloves, I got it on my own hands from massaging him to relieve his constant itching. It gives off a sickening, nauseating odor.

The doctor took our family medical history to see if Samuel had a naturally strong constitution. This helps him decide which medication to fight the infection with. He warned us of possible damage to Samuel's vital organs, but we agreed to allow the strong drugs. What else could we do? The itching was unbearable.

Lorene: Another crisis. They paged us in the chapel: "Please return to ICU." Now it's his scalp, which looks like it might die. Big clots of blood beneath his scalp are turning dark. Doctors tell us that when veins are damaged, they are prone to clotting. The blood flows freely into Samuel's scalp but not out. This causes swelling and blood clots. His scalp is turning black — he may lose it. So they want to use leeches to suck out the bad blood.

Oba: They invited Lorene and me to watch as Dr. Yen put two of these little three-inch leeches on Samuel's scalp. Leeches are flattish, live in water or moist earth. Their mouths have three, small, white teeth which act as saws, making a wound so they can suck the blood. Curious nurses who had never seen this before crowded into the room.

We watched, amazed, as these tiny creatures drained the dark pockets in Samuel's scalp, then fell off, bloated with the blood. As they dropped off, an ICU technician picked them up with tweezers and dropped them into a paper cup of peroxide. They told me leeches seldom leave scars and are painless due to a self-producing anesthesia. Am I beginning to sound like a doctor?

WEDNESDAY, AUGUST 28, 1991

Oba: Paul called with more bad news: "A speeder just ran over Boots." Boots, my prized Australian Blue Heeler who read my mind before I said a word. It's not right to grieve over a dog when your son is so near death, but one grief compounds another. Is there no end?

Lorene. Three more hours of surgery for Samuel today: Skin grafts to cover raw tissue and more leeches. It has gotten to be a ritual. They take him to surgery, bed and all, but first they disconnect the respirator and use a hand pump in its place. It has a different hum. We know when he's out of surgery — we hear the same hum, then a different tone as the respirator is plugged into an outlet. Also, we know the sound of the fan inside the special air bed. So we listen as he leaves his room, listen as he returns. Did he survive? Is he okay?

Dr. Yen called: "Fifty-fifty chance of saving the scalp." The waiting is hard. Please, Lord, give us patience. We know they're doing all they can.

As we waited, a nearby patient came out of her room to make a phone call. I remembered her from yesterday, when she acted as if she wanted to speak to me. This time she introduced herself and said, "I know by your dress you're religious. May I talk with you?"

She said she lived in Springfield, where she worked for the Illinois Department of Revenue.

She was here for heat stroke. Got exhausted while volunteering in the food stands at the Air Rendezvous last week. She said she was depressed, spiritually and physically, and felt that she had been doing too much for others and not looking out for herself. So, she told God she was "resigning" from helping others. She promised God she'd still go to church but she wanted no demands put on her.

Then she asked whom we were visiting. When I told her about Samuel, she said, "Oh, I'm so sorry. My problems are trivial!"

Oba: Doctors tried something new to get more oxygen into Samuel to speed up the healing, especially his scalp. It's called the Hyperbaric Oxygen (HBO) chamber. They seal the patient inside this cylinder and use pressure to force oxygen into his lungs. But it scares Samuel; makes him feel caged in.

I can see the terror in his eyes. When they took him out tonight, he threw up, and Dr. Russell said, "No more; it's too hard on him. We'll try something else."

Oh, what pain to see a loved one suffer. We could tell it was hard on the nurses to seal him in that chamber every eight hours. We thought nurses didn't cry, but we learned better. Oh, if Samuel could sit beside me in the buggy one more time and go for a ride, like to the schoolhouse last week. What simple pleasures we take for granted until they're gone.

THURSDAY, AUGUST 29, 1991

Lorene: You don't get your rest trying to sleep on the floor or in a recliner. I was up at 3:00 a.m. to check on Samuel — resting good. All night I kept repeating, "Peace I leave with you, my peace I give to you; not as the world giveth, give I unto you." (John 14:27)

Oba: Larry Neuman from Chatham said he felt led to come to the hospital this morning. He and Donna are genuine friends, here every other night, always bringing food or something. He has enough to do this time of year without looking after us. With his son and brother, he cultivates lots of land (makes my farm look like a vegetable garden).

But the Neumans know suffering. In 1974, Donna lay critically ill for sixty-two days in a hospital with a ruptured liver, caused by a fall. I was glad he was coming today, for I needed a ride home to the farm. I hadn't left the hospital for a week, and I had got word the children were having problems. Nothing major, but I needed to talk to them.

I had dreaded this day. I shuddered at the thought of seeing the barnyard again, of reliving the accident for which I feel responsible. Larry and I said little in the car; I cried most of the way.

At the farm, I tried to focus on the children and the future rather than the horror of the past. I got them all together and we talked for an hour and a half. It was good for us. I told them how pleased I was with what they were doing, especially Paul, who had quit his job to be their dad. John, William, Rosanna, and Steven are still in school, and although I know it's hard, I encouraged them to concentrate on their studies. Steven, the "round-up boy," hitches the school buggy each morning. William's job is to sweep the barn and feed the cows. John looks out for the ponies and colts. Philip and Mary Anna, both preschoolers, stay at home. David, Duane, and Chris are old enough to help with crops. Susanna helps her sister-in-law care for month-old Marneta, and also helps to cook, wash, mend, and sew.

I am proud of them all.

Larry waited patiently in his car, enjoying some homemade peach pie that David ran out to him.

By dark, we were back in Springfield. How long would this vigil last?

3. "But, Dad, it's a good arm!"

FRIDAY, AUGUST 30, 1991

Lorene: Today Helen Smith was discharged. Before leaving, Helen told me, "I know you people have your own customs and ways, but here are my work and home numbers. Call me anytime for transportation, meals, even a visit in my home to rest."

Samuel coughed most of the night. They moved two recliners into his room so we can sleep there instead of in the lounge. At best, we catnapped. Samuel often wakes and whispers in German, "Mom, Dad are you there?" We say yes, we're here, and he goes back to sleep. But only for an hour or so. His voice is so frail.

Lewis Chupp called with bad news from home. Their son Glen broke his wrist when a pony ran away with his cart. Ruby Yoder broke her ankle in a fall. Susie Yoder passed away. And in a freak accident, a baby in the community fell headlong into a diaper pail and drowned. We've been so close to death that news like this is even more frightening. I hum, "One Day at a Time, Sweet Jesus."

SATURDAY, AUGUST 31, 1991

Oba: Feeling we needed one night's sleep in a real bed, I called Helen Smith: "Were you serious, inviting us to your home? And you just out of the hospital?" She insisted we come and she picked us up at 10:00 p.m.

Lorene: Although it was late when we got to Helen's, her Mom, Rosella, fixed a meal — our first home cooking in over a week. She baked a peach pie, mashed some potatoes, fried some chicken, and warmed over a pizza and vegetables in her microwave (first one I'd ever seen up close). We showered and I shampooed my hair. I thought I'd broken Helen's hairdryer, but it only came unplugged.

Oba: For a few hours, we soaked up Helen's hospitality, but I still worried about Samuel. As we went to bed, Helen reminded us that the hospital was only fifteen minutes away. The bed was very comfortable, but thoughts of dear Samuel blocked sound sleep.

SUNDAY, SEPTEMBER 1, 1991

Lorene: It's Sunday, and lots of company has come. Our children alone fill the small waiting room near the ICU. Each visitor gives us a lift. I took little Marneta, Samuel's month-old niece, in to see him.

Helen Smith took our laundry home. She promised Samuel that since he was so sick on his birthday, she'd come after work on Friday with a surprise, something he could look forward to all week. A friend of Helen's came too, and insisted on giving us some cash for food and incidentals.

Samuel developed a stomach ulcer and was sick all day.

Oba: About 10:30 tonight, Samuel said his back felt like it was on fire. Lorene reached under him, and the sheet was bloody. He was bleeding from his right arm. Four nurses worked with him. He started to turn white. A doctor came and somehow the five of them got the bleeding stopped by sewing up an artery that had broken open.

They also gave him two units of blood to replace what he had lost. Since there wasn't time to give him anesthesia, he suffered terribly; I held him, tried to reassure him. He kept coughing; a nurse suctioned his mouth. They also used more leeches.

MONDAY, SEPTEMBER 2, 1991

Lorene: Samuel was in surgery four hours to try to save his arm. They grafted a blood vessel from one of his legs. We won't know for a couple of days whether it works or not.

A vanload of friends came three hundred miles from near Bloomfield, Iowa, where we once lived.

It was a sad reunion.

WEDNESDAY, SEPTEMBER 4, 1991

Lorene: Samuel wouldn't eat all day — his throat is too sore. He's restless, itchy.

We received a letter and offering from the First Christian Church in Sullivan today. Many prayers have been said for us. We are overwhelmed with gratitude.

More surgery — Samuel's left arm is causing problems.

Oba: At night, Samuel asks me to play the harmonica. I'm self-taught, but he likes it. I have our German hymnal. The children also brought me our *Church and Sunday School Hymnal,* which has some of his favorite Protestant hymns and choruses, such as "Amazing Grace" and "This World Is Not My Home." He smiled through his pain.

Late at night, I was reading a Gideon Bible by the light of one small lamp when Sister Veronica came in. She was a great comfort. To me, people like her are messengers from

God, and the Bible is the verbal presence of God.

THURSDAY, SEPTEMBER 5, 1991

Oba: Our son Joseph is fifteen today, but we won't see him. We heard that someone had criticized us for spending too much time at the hospital and neglecting the others. Oh, how this hurts. It's not that we love Samuel more — he just needs us more. We'd do the same for any of our children. As Psalms 127:3 says, "Lo, children are a heritage of the Lord."

It looks now as if the doctors will be able to save only half of Samuel's scalp. And his right arm? No one knows. Right now, they're treating his high fever with ice packs.

FRIDAY, SEPTEMBER 6, 1991

Lorene: Samuel gave us a bad scare this morning; he started breathing very hard. Penny ran in, talked to him, and tried to get him to say something to make sure he was still with us. She called for help — Dr. Russell and Dr. Yen.

Oba: As they consulted around his bed, Samuel appeared to fall asleep. But we've seen him pretend before, so he could listen. Dr. Russell said we needed to make a decision: unless they amputate Samuel's left arm, he doubts if Samuel will live much longer. The yeast fungus continues to spread, and if it gets out of control, there will be no hope.

Dr. Russell explained: "Both arms are crying, 'Heal me.' His legs are crying, 'Heal me.' Likewise his scalp. Ordinarily, we get a patient with one or two major injuries. But Samuel's torn up all over. His little body can't handle it. Each day, he grows weaker. One source of infection has to be removed immediately, and we think it's this arm." Dr. Yen agreed.

I looked at Lorene. Without discussion, we knew what we had to do. I nodded Yes, because a lump in my throat blocked my words. So we signed the permissions.

I asked if I should tell Samuel. Dr. Russell said not now, that he has enough to worry him. I moved to his side and said, "Samuel, your doctors are here." He opened his eyes and whispered, "Yes, I know. I heard them talking. But, Dad, it's a good arm — look, it's going to be all right. Please, please, please don't let them!"

What could I say? Dear Lord, show me the way.

We followed Samuel to the surgery door, one of the longest, hardest walks of our lives. The nurses cried with us.

Lorene: He was in surgery for three and a half hours. We hurried to the chapel to wait. We enjoy the quiet here. Oba says that it's loud with quietness! The twelve short pews seat about forty. Although we worship in plain homes, the soft colors here soothe me. A stained-glass figure of Jesus looks down from the altar, lighted from the back. He lifts his right hand in benediction: "I am the light of the world; he that followeth me shall have the light of life." Figures of Matthew, Mark, Luke, and John — authors of the four Gospels — are on either side. And there's a prayer request lectern, where you can leave handwritten praises and petitions. I often read some of them, as a reminder that sometime, somewhere, pain comes to everyone.

Still more bad news from home: Dan Miller, my childhood bishop, died unexpectedly.

Oba: Paul called from home: "Dad, I don't want to worry you, but after Boots got killed, one of our Holsteins died. Found her in the pasture. And that good mare, Ann, you bought before the accident? Well, she died too. I have no idea why. Another thing: the motor blew up on the skid steer we use to load manure. And you know we have lots of rust in our water. Well, some of it must have broken loose and clogged the pipes, because we have no water."

I felt like giving up. Instead, I remembered a helpful poem:

O Master, let me walk with thee
In lowly paths of service free . . .
Help me bear the fret of care
In peace that only thou canst give.
(Washington Gladden, 1879)

Lorene: They brought Samuel back to the ICU at 2:00 p.m. We braced ourselves to see him; he looked so different with one arm gone!

As word spread, family and friends poured in. There's not room for everyone in the waiting area. While we all waited, Barbara Sue Kuhns and Barbara Ann Miller sang two songs. It was past midnight when Samuel finally woke up. His first words were, "Is Helen's surprise here?" He remembered her promise. And sure enough it was — a giant poster-size birthday card signed by employees at the Department of Revenue, plus about fifty one-dollar bills taped to the card. This was the first time I'd seen him smile since the accident.

SUNDAY, SEPTEMBER 8, 1991

Lorene: Since losing his arm, Samuel has been on a rollercoaster — fever up and down. Lots of pain medicine, such as intravenous amphotericin (Dr. Graham says some call it "ampho*terrible*").

Dr. Graham thinks we're gaining on the yeast infection, but the horrible itching won't stop. What's it like to hurt and itch at the same time? I get so little rest. "Mom, Mom, Mom," Samuel cries if I'm out of his sight. Oba and I are both about worn out. Plus we're concerned for the children at home. Please, Lord, watch over them and give us *geduld* (patience).

Oba: I didn't know one could function on so little sleep. As soon as we close our eyes, it seems Samuel needs something. And it scares him if he wakes up and we're asleep.

When our friends leave, we get so lonesome. During the day, the hospital bustles with activity — florists bringing flowers, patients checking in and out, nurses serving meals, student residents on the elevators, housekeepers mopping and cleaning, doctors making their rounds, customers in the gift shop. Then night settles in, and most of the visitors leave. The lights dim. The halls grow silent.

Sometimes I go to a window and look out over the city — the lights, the traffic, people going home to their families, enjoying their suppers, homework, then safe in bed. A plane with its red lights blinking descends to nearby Capital Airport. And then a siren pierces the night and an ambulance unloads at the emergency room. Who's sick now, or hurt? Will they live? And their loved ones — do they know, are they with them?

I relive our own frantic drive to the hospital a week ago last Friday. Did it really happen? Is this a bad dream? When morning comes, will everything go back to the way it was? Will the boys and I head to the barn to milk, while Lorene starts breakfast?

Sometimes at night, you hear a patient scream out in pain, and you get to thinking that this is a house of death and everyone's dying!

MONDAY, SEPTEMBER 9, 1991

Oba: Tonight was the worst ever. Rain, thunder and lightning, when all of a sudden Samuel screamed, "Get me out of here! See those snakes crawling on the ceiling! They're coming down to get me! Help me, help me!" Nurses rushed in to help us quiet him.

By now, these nurses are like our sisters. They tell us that Samuel is reacting to all the strong medicine given to dull the pain where his arm was amputated, plus the powerful drugs to kill the yeast fungus. They stroke his brow as he settles down.

Lorene: We spent most of the night trying to calm Samuel and relieve the itching, which made him thrash from one side of the bed to the other. We bathed and oiled and rubbed and powdered him. Finally, he slept. I've lost count of the blood he's received. Seventy units at least. Tonight I'm so tired I can't think.

TUESDAY, SEPTEMBER 10, 1991

Oba: Today I was asked to meet with a social worker. She shuffled her papers, ill at ease, until finally she said, "We thought you'd want to know what it's costing here in the ICU, so you can start planning. It's many thousands of dollars a week. That's not counting the surgeons and radiologists." I'm sure my face turned white.

Then she added, kindly, "The hospital is more concerned with Samuel's health than money. But still, you need to know. I understand you have no insurance?" I nodded, explaining that we Amish don't insure anything — our health, our houses, livestock, crops, nothing. When an Amish family needs help, our churches take up relief offerings or assess each family

She replied, "I'm afraid this is going to be more than your church, or any church, can do alone." Panic gripped me. Would we indeed lose everything?

WEDNESDAY, SEPTEMBER 11, 1991

Lorene: What a difference two days can make! Samuel's shoulder is healing, and Dr. Graham says we're gaining on the fungus. But he's still itchy. We sat Samuel up in a chair, and they removed the catheter. One small step. Best of all, they moved him from the ICU to the Plastic Surgery Unit on the second floor, Room B-214. With a full bath! Now we have more privacy to bathe and a place to store our change of clothes. But they warned us to expect more surgeries — trimming his scalp, changing the casts, dressing the shoulder stump where they removed his arm, etc. It's hard on the new nurses, coping with such a sick patient.

Oba: A reporter from the *State Journal-Register* was here. She wants to write a feature story about Samuel. She said many people in Springfield are asking about him and want to do whatever they can to help. This is the work of Helen Smith, who has been making phone calls around town and has arranged for a "Friends of Samuel Herschberger" bank account to receive contributions.

All this makes me dizzy. I had no idea Helen, a recent patient herself, was doing such a thing. I hardly know how to handle the news. I like to do for others, but I'm not used to others doing for me. I'm more comfortable being on the giving end.

THURSDAY, SEPTEMBER 12, 1991

Oba: I couldn't believe what I saw on the front page of the *State Journal-Register* — a long story about Samuel with a big headline, "Amish Boy's Injuries Evoke Aid from the Modern World." It told all about the accident and how people were helping us. I appreciate this, but oh, the publicity scares me; it is so foreign to our way of life. I could hardly finish the article. It was like reliving a nightmare. Seeing the story in print reminded me that it really happened. But I'm not ready to accept it. Maybe I'm in some kind of denial.

By noon, the hospital phones were ringing, callers wanting to talk to me, offering to help.

FRIDAY, SEPTEMBER 13, 1991

Oba: More phone calls, some requesting interviews. Lots of get-well cards, including one from basketball star Michael Jordan of the Chicago Bulls (who also tried to call, but we missed connections). The Associated Press released Samuel's story, too. Many newspapers and radio stations picked it up. What will my people think? That I've lost faith in our church's ability to help with these big hospital bills? That I'm turning to the outside world? God knows my motives. I never wanted my name in print. But these last few weeks have shown me there are many good and Godly people, people who use different words to describe their religious beliefs but share a common vision. I guess I grew up rather sheltered, unaware that other faiths are also sincere and committed.

Lorene: Yesterday afternoon I went home for the first time in three weeks and spent the night. I didn't really want to, but I thought it was good for the children. I helped with chores again, and the next morning six ladies came to help sew. We cut and made seven pairs of pants. I took them back to the hospital to hem and make buttonholes.

I like to keep busy with my hands. From the first day here, I've had my crochet bag, working on little things. Helps to pass the time, relieves my mind. I also started keeping a journal the day after the accident, a big tablet I write in every day. Or sometimes at night when I'm lonely. And if I think of it, I ask our visitors to sign it. I must have over two hundred names — twenty-six visitors, just today. Oba says he will not read any more newspaper stories about the accident. Maybe it's his way of pretending it never happened. But I read all of them and save the clippings for a scrapbook, which I want to make when we take Samuel home.

SATURDAY, SEPTEMBER 14, 1991

Oba: I'm forty-three years old today, and our Mary Anna will be four tomorrow. I would have paid no attention, but Helen Smith and her mother, Rosella, cooked a surprise birthday supper and gave me a watch.

4. Loving Hearts, Helping Hands

MONDAY, SEPTEMBER 16, 1991

Lorene: Good news came today! The Sisters at St. Mary's Hospital in Decatur (Illinois) will pay our bill there in full — over $4,000! That was for Samuel's emergency care. And after Friday, we won't need to pay rent for his Kinair bed. The rental company saw the article in the paper and is contributing the use of the bed. And a blood test showed that Samuel is at last free from the yeast fungus, although Dr. Graham wants to continue medication for awhile. Now, maybe his scalp will heal. However, we can expect more surgeries. Number eight today.

Tom Gale brought a big sign his wife made at school — "Get well, Samuel, from Mrs. Gale's 4th grade." They're from Lovington, Illinois, and Tom sells us fertilizer and other farm products. He's always bringing something for our youngsters, such as candy.

WEDNESDAY, SEPTEMBER 18, 1991

Oba: More mail, cards, and phone calls. I've agreed to do interviews, but at our request the hospital has asked news personnel not to photograph us. I have such mixed feelings — gratitude for the donations pouring into the bank fund, but uneasiness with the publicity. The TV program "Rescue 911" has queried, but we don't want a camera crew at the farm taking the children's minds off their schoolwork. Also *People* magazine called, but I said no, for that would mean photographs. The Springfield newspaper, whose story started all the support, has never asked us for a photo; they respect our beliefs about that. We need help, but I'll never exploit Samuel's suffering.

Lorene: Another big step — we took Samuel for a ride in a wheelchair on the hospital grounds! We're such a familiar sight around here with our homemade dresses and bonnets and plain-front trousers that people often ask questions. And I don't mind — I like to talk. Children sometimes ask Oba, "Why do you wear those strange-looking clothes?" He has friendly answers — "So I won't get sunburned," or, "I'd look funnier if I didn't wear something!"

I sew all of our clothing except socks, gloves, underwear, and the like. I guess our homemade clothing is one way of saying who we are. Helen Smith said it was our dress that attracted her. Our churches don't put out mailings or send missionaries, so maybe what we wear is a quiet statement of who we are.

It's not easy to sew, mend, and wash for thirteen children. But I grew up that way. I'm one of nineteen children, including my half-sisters and brothers. That's a lot of sewing!

We wear solid colors — no patterns. We prefer plain, quiet shades of brown, blue, gray, teal, plum, and black. For Sunday, the men and boys wear white shirts. To church we women wear white, organdy capes over our long dresses, plus a white, organdy veil or cap on our heads (except single girls, who wear black prayer caps), tied with a ribbon under the chin. In public, we wear a bonnet over the veil.

Oba: Lorene makes clothes for me and the boys. We wear no-fly pants, joined with four buttons at the front and two in the back to suspenders. We never wear coveralls or bib overalls. Our shirts are pocketless. Lorene also sews our winter coats and heavy jackets. For dress, men wear hats with wide brims and a flat crown. Even the smallest boys. She uses snaps for everyday jackets, hook-and-eyes for Sunday coats. We have an expression for what the non-Amish wear: we call them "English clothes."

THURSDAY, SEPTEMBER 19, 1991

Lorene: Samuel was restless last night but slept better after we moved him to a recliner. Here on the second floor, we met Chaplain Dave Nicholson, who is assigned to our wing and sees us about four times a week. It's comforting to know that the chaplains carry beepers (another first for me), and when on call, they are never more than ten minutes from the hospital. Now that Samuel's out of ICU, we hold morning devotions in his room, instead of the chapel.

A state policeman, a veteran of the Gulf War, came today and gave Samuel some pictures made in Saudi Arabia, plus a medal and hat he got overseas. I had to sit down and cry, that a busy person like him would visit a little boy he doesn't even know.

Oba: Gifts and cards are overrunning Samuel's room. I've been told that one day it took four employees to open the mail at the Cook Street branch of First National Bank, where the bank account for Samuel is. We've agreed that they will handle all these funds. I won't touch them. And our church leaders will oversee another fund that has been established — the Jonathan Creek Church District fund at Heartland Federal Savings & Loan in Sullivan.

Somehow, word has gotten out that Lorene and I eat from Samuel's tray because we can't afford to buy food. Often, he doesn't feel like eating. If so, we share his food, which otherwise would be thrown away. But it's not because we're so hard up for money. It's that we can't stand to see anything wasted. We live close to the soil, and I know the work it takes to raise food. I know what it's like to go to the barn to milk at 5:00 a.m. when it's below zero and the wind cuts like a knife. So how could we throw away even one carton of milk or an uneaten slice of toast?

FRIDAY, SEPTEMBER 20, 1991

Oba: A man in the visitor's lounge was surprised to learn that the Amish are Christians. I guess our beards and plain dress made him think of Old Testament patriarchs! I explained that although the Amish date back to the Protestant Reformation, our early leaders felt reformers such as Zwingli and Luther didn't go far enough. We come from the Anabaptist tradition; that is, our founders "rebaptized" converts who had been baptized as infants. They felt a person should be baptized only when he or she was old enough to decide.

Menno Simons, born in 1496, helped establish the Mennonite Church. Later, Jacob Amman, feeling even the Mennonites were too liberal, formed the Old Order Amish and renounced violence as a way to settle differences. My family, whose roots are in Germany and Switzerland, still belongs to the Old Order, the strictest element of the Amish faith.

The man asked if we serve in the Armed Forces. I explained that although we are conscientious objectors, during wartime our young men do give two years of compulsory service in hospitals and state institutions. As I see it, fighting can never solve our differences. My boys own guns, and when they're about fifteen I send them to safety clinics, but their guns are not intended for use in war. We use guns to hunt game. I hunt only for food, not sport. Life

— even animal life — is very sacred to me.

SATURDAY, SEPTEMBER 21, 1991

Oba: We fixed Samuel a big cup of soda and crushed ice, then wheeled him to a wing where he could watch the airplanes circling over Springfield and coming in for landings at Capital Airport. I told him how Jerry Coleman of Chatham had asked members of the Illinois Pilots Association to donate their planes and time for a "fly-in," giving rides for $8 for adults and $5 for children, to raise money for Samuel. As we watched the planes, Samuel couldn't believe they were doing it for him! He's never flown in a plane. In fact, no one in our family has.

SUNDAY, SEPTEMBER 22, 1991

Oba: I went home today and attended worship services at the home of Paul Yoder. I'm not sure how much attention I paid, for I still feel dazed. It was time for Ordung Gma, the second Sunday before communion, and the themes focused on sacrifice and love. I always thrill when we sing the "Loblied," a traditional German hymn of praise. It's sung at every service, including funerals and weddings. It reminds us our faith never changes, no matter what:

O Gott Fater, wir loben dich,
Und deine Gute preisen;
Daz du dich, o Serr, gnadiglich,
Un uns neu hast bewiesen.
Und hast uns, Herr, zusammen g'fuhrt
Uns zu ermahnen durch dein Wort,
Gib uns Genad ZU diefem.

Loosely translated, here's the hymn in English:

O God the Father, we praise thee
For thy wondrous works,
That you, O God, in your kindness,
You have shown us mercy,
And, O God, have brought us together,
And reminded us through your Word
Of the grace bestowed on us.

Lorene: Oba and I are eating better. Our appetites seem to be coming back. For a while, the thought of food almost sickened us. Three times a week, someone has been bringing us a restaurant menu, and they send whatever we order, at no cost — the very best of vegetables, meats, and desserts. It's always more than we can eat, so we send leftovers home to the children. At first we said no, but the people at the hospital insisted. We asked who's doing this for us, but they won't say.

Oba: When I got back to the hospital, Lorene handed me a newspaper. I couldn't believe the write-up about the fly-in yesterday; it raised nearly $7,000. The volunteer pilots flew 1,500 passengers and turned away another thousand. One of them was a first-time flyer, an eighty-five-year-old woman. And the employees of First National Bank held a bake sale in one of the hangars, raising nearly $1,200. They started selling at 6:00 a.m. and planned to close at noon, but people kept coming. One lady, a caterer from Sherman, donated $400 from her sales; she remembered the help she got sixteen years ago when her own son was paralyzed in a swimming accident. Also, the Revenue Recreation Club staged music, clowns, and food. Behind much of this wonderful outpouring of support was the energetic Helen Smith, who four weeks ago told us she had "resigned" from helping people.

Samuel enjoyed the rare photograph of his aunt, Mattie Miller, walking across the runway carrying doughnuts, pies, cakes, cinnamon rolls, caramel tea rings, bread, and rolls. She and Anna Rotaberger of Arthur brought a vanload of Amish pastries for the sale. (She didn't know a photographer snapped her picture when she wasn't looking.)

MONDAY, SEPTEMBER 23, 1991

Lorene: Christina Miller, a local teenager, comes often to visit. She says she always wanted to meet an Amish family. I'm afraid she thinks we're better than we really are, but I've told her several times that we're just like anyone else. She's fascinated that we speak English and German (or Pennsylvania Dutch, as Oba calls it — a mix of German, English, and Swiss words).

Helen Smith and Debbie Owens brought Samuel a new bicycle. They wouldn't say who donated it. Samuel wants it at the foot of his bed where he can see it. We're running out of space. Some fourth-graders from Chandler, Arizona, sent him a packet of letters. Someone else sent him a teddy bear that plays sixteen songs when you press a button in his chest. Oba laid it on the end of his bed where he can press the musical button with the cast of his right leg.

Oba: Today, for the first time, Samuel talked to his mom about the accident — how he got off the tractor to get his hat, got caught in the PTO, and then freed himself. But he couldn't remember being caught again. He remembers the siren and lots of people around him. I think it does him good to talk about it.

THURSDAY, SEPTEMBER 26, 1991

Oba: Surgery again yesterday — the tenth time, I believe. This one lasted four hours. It's been five weeks since we came here; a family member has been with Samuel every day and night.

Mary Bulpitt, a member of the Springfield Precious Moments Club, came to visit Samuel today, but he was too weak to talk. Mary's organization sent us $100 for phone, postage, and transportation for our children's visits to the hospital. She gave Samuel a four-inch Precious Moments figurine, a small boy titled "Jesus Loves Me." Mary said that in the past twelve years she has helped to care for and bury a total of ten close friends and relatives, making her sensitive to others' hurts. Next month she's going to the Precious Moments Chapel near Carthage, Missouri, to ask if they can help with our expenses.

I understand that the bank fund is near $75,000. Dear God, thank you for all the wonderful people who are helping us. Someday, in some way, I hope we can repay them.

FRIDAY, SEPTEMBER 27, 1991

Oba: My brother, Monroe, a contractor for over thirty-five years, made some sketches, showing how we might remodel our house. We'll need more room for Samuel when we go home, and better heat. Otherwise, I don't see how we can manage, especially with only one bath.

My back aches; one night when we had only one recliner, we took turns sleeping on the floor. After five weeks, you miss your bed. But I know our discomfort is nothing compared to Samuel's, so I even hesitate to mention it.

They started physical therapy with Samuel today. He can move one finger, bend one knee, and swivel one ankle. Since therapy, if it's done right, must push Samuel to the point of pain, they think we shouldn't watch. But we insisted, so we can learn to do it at home. They were right — it hurt to watch.

Lorene: We went to look at the Ronald McDonald House near St. John's Hospital. Oba and I could stay there nights, sleep in real beds, and do some home cooking. It's a godsend for out-of-town parents, but I don't feel right being separated from Samuel. So we came back to Memorial Medical Center.

THURSDAY, OCTOBER 3, 1991

Lorene: Kenny Golden from Havana, Illinois, came by to

encourage Samuel. When Kenny was about fifteen, he lost an arm when he came in contact with a live electrical wire. He left a note saying, “Keep going, and don’t feel sorry for yourself.” A group of teachers brought cards from the Little Flower School in Springfield, and a Shriner came to offer help from the Hospital for Crippled Children in St. Louis.

Samuel needs these boosts. He’s itchy again with a rash and seems depressed. He cries easily and complains that the food is no good here. His one good arm looks so thin and the skin is beginning to peel. He said he wished he had lost a leg, instead of his arm, and that he’ll never get to ride his new bike. So while he was asleep, we hid it in the bathroom behind the shower curtain. He has been so patient, so brave, that it hurts to see him like this. But the nurses say that it’s normal for a critically injured child.

SUNDAY, OCTOBER 6, 1991

Lorene: A rough night for me. We always have lots of company on Sundays, but when they leave I grow homesick. If I go home, I feel guilty for neglecting Samuel. If I stay here, I feel guilty for neglecting those at home. So after midnight, I wrote in my journal:

> *Greetings in Jesus’ name. Here I am in the wee hours of the morning. I started crying and can’t stop. I want to go home and be a whole family again! Help me, God, I want to go home. I want to hold Marneta and Mary Anna and all the rest so tight. I love them so much. I want to cook and wash clothes and milk our cows — just a normal life. At times, I wonder if Samuel will ever be well again. I’m not a good example, like people think. I’m just a poor human being who makes mistakes.*

Dear God, why did this happen to us? Forgive me for asking why. I know You're with us through it all.

MONDAY, OCTOBER 7, 1991

Oba: We had visitors today from Atlanta, Illinois, about thirty-five miles north of Springfield. Nancy Vannoy and her son Devin, fifteen, told us an amazing story that boosted our spirits tremendously.

In August, 1978, when Devin was two years old, he fell into a grain auger. It severed his right arm in two places — above the elbow and at the shoulder — and cut off his left arm just above the elbow. He was rushed to Abraham Lincoln Memorial Hospital in Lincoln, then to St. John's Hospital in Springfield. It was one of the hottest days of that summer, and four hours passed before they found the severed body parts. (They had fallen into a receptacle for chopped corn, which served to insulate and keep them cool.)

Finally, five hours after the accident, Devin went into surgery, which lasted thirteen hours.

At first doctors thought Devin's arm fragments were too damaged to reattach, but Dr. Allen L. Van Beek and our Dr. Russell volunteered to try. The operation was a success, and Devin became the first known bilateral (two limbs) replant in the world! Fortunately, there was no massive infection.

Then in his early teens, doctors used the Ilizarov External Fixator to lengthen Devin's right arm by twelve inches.

Lorene: Nancy is our messenger from heaven. Dr. Russell had mentioned this "fixator" as a way to lengthen Samuel's right leg, but we had no idea he had successfully used it on someone right here in central Illinois.

Nancy talked to us for a long time, giving valuable practical advice. Devin, somewhat like Samuel, had received all kinds of publicity — newspaper articles from England, Germany, and Africa. Also, friends put on ten benefits to help pay his medical bills. Dr. Van Beek came to one of the benefits, which featured a big barrel for donations. He dropped this note, written on the back of his business card, into the barrel: "To a concerned community and a small child: My services are donated." He also attended Devin's Eighth Grade commencement.

Nancy warned us of how a few people react when you get so much recognition: "Some become jealous, wondering why they aren't written up in the papers or given donations." She also repeated some of the thoughtless remarks people had made. One person told them that if they had enough faith, God would heal Devin instantly. This made them feel guilty.

Another said, "The way Devin looks with his mangled arms, wouldn't it be wiser to amputate them, since the new prostheses are so efficient?" Nancy explained that a prosthesis may be effective, but it's also cold and unfeeling: "With no arms, Devin could never hug me or his Dad again." As Devin's arms were healing, he tried to hug his family with his legs, so strong was his desire to feel and touch.

I hope no one's ever jealous of the donations we've received. Who would want to endure all Samuel's suffering and our anguish just to get help with medical bills.

6. Going Home

WEDNESDAY, OCTOBER 9, 1991

Lorene: The doctors say that if I learn to change bandages and give IVs, we can go home soon. Praise God!

I've been making hot pads for people we've met up here. Oba took some to the ICU nurses, who seemed appreciative.

We took Samuel outside this afternoon. He was in a good mood and laughed with the nurses. When one of them asked if he needed anything, he said, "A new head!"

Samuel and Larry Neuman joke about who makes the best tractors — John Deere or International. Samuel insists it's John Deere. Tonight Larry brought him a sack of candy corn and a sack of jelly beans. Samuel said, "That's the kind of corn and beans you raise with an International!"

Although Samuel's gaining strength, the nights are still long. He asked me to lie beside him and rub his arm, but then my arm fell asleep and I moved to a chair. Oba was up and down all night.

Oba: I just met the woman who's been donating big bags of food for us three times a week. I caught up with her in the hallway and asked her name, but she refused. She explained, "I'm trying to teach my children to help others, without expecting something back. And had I stopped to talk with you, I was afraid I might start crying and upset Samuel."

SATURDAY, OCTOBER 12, 1991

Oba: In the waiting area, someone asked why we Amish accept rides in cars but don't own or drive them. I explained it's because our lifestyle encourages togetherness. Cars not only take you to a distant place, they also take you *away* from something — your family. If we owned cars, some of us would be on the road all the time.

There's nothing "sinful" about a car. A speeding ambulance helped save Samuel's life. In a buggy, we'd never have made it. And when the children come to the hospital to visit, we hire a van or maybe a neighbor brings them. I guess there are twenty drivers in the Arthur area who operate vans for the Amish, charging about 50¢ per mile. Some of these are vans that transport Amish men who work at jobs away from their farms. One joke has it that some day, 80 percent of the world will be Amish, and the other 20 percent will be driving them around!

Columnist Ann Landers once wrote, "It's often easier and less hazardous to reach one's destination by the back roads rather than the busy highways." I agree.

We feel the same about television. We want our children to interact with each other, to carry on conversations. We want them to enjoy good times on their own, rather than watching someone else have fun. If we had a TV and I watched sports three or four hours a day, how could I do my farm work, have time to hunt and fish with my boys, and take them ice-skating and to horse sales?

Lorene: In surgery today they trimmed Samuel's scalp, but half of it is dead. The leeches helped but not 100 percent. In a few months, they'll try a technique to expand the part of his scalp that's still alive. Doctors also put a catheter through his chest to a main artery so we can do IVs when we go home.

TUESDAY, OCTOBER 15, 1991

Oba: The doctors have said they will release Samuel on one condition: that we install a telephone. Memorial Home Care doesn't want us out on the farm at night with no way to call for help. This may be a problem, because we Amish don't usually have phones except in businesses. We apply the same standard to telephones that we do to other conveniences like cars or TVs — What's best for the family? Think of all the incoming calls for twelve children! We'd never eat a meal in peace.

Lorene: The newspaper says the fund at First National Bank has gone over $100,000 and is still growing. Helen Smith was here today when one of the hospital's financial officers was reviewing our bill with Oba. I'm sure it's much more than the bank fund. Helen asked if the hospital would settle for a lesser amount if we made one cash payment. He said he'd look into it. That's not counting the doctors.

Oba: We're beginning to pack and say our good-byes. Unit 2-B has become almost like home in some ways. Tomorrow a truck will take the toys, balloons, bicycle, wheelchair, and the thousands of greeting cards we have received, as well as a new waterbed for Samuel, a recliner, and a dresser for his medical supplies. I wonder how we can find a place for everything.

The nurses have been so good to us, working around all the mementos that make Samuel's room look like a storage closet. One nurse explained that they often make videos of children who've been traumatized and show them to their classmates before the children return to school, so they won't be teased.

If Samuel's friends tease him, it won't be because the

Amish don't teach them better. We rear our children to accept others the way they are.

THURSDAY, OCTOBER 17, 1991

Oba: We have been promised the use of a temporary phone, a cellular one, when we get home. We're still waiting for church approval of a permanent one.

We met our new home-care nurses. They watched me change Samuel's leg dressings and Lorene do his IVs. We passed the exam!

Last night, Lorene dreamed that Samuel died. I think we're uneasy about how we'll manage out in the country, seventy miles from his doctors. And our drafty heating system — what if Samuel gets pneumonia or something this winter? It's so snug and secure here in the hospital.

Displayed in various places around the hospital is Memorial's Statement of Purpose. It reads as if it were written for us:

> *To care for life's precious gift of health is a calling of the highest order.*
> *We recognize the vulnerability that accompanies fear and hope.*
> *We accept the responsibility entrusted to us every day, to serve humanity.*

Lorene: The day we had waited for! Larry Neuman was driving us home in his van. Just as I had dreaded, reporters and cameramen were all outside the hospital. We didn't want our pictures in the paper, but hospital officials said they couldn't control cameras on the streets since that's public property. They offered to let us leave by a rear door, but Oba said it would look ungrateful if we slipped out. So we decided to go through with it.

One of the last to tell us good-bye was Della, the cleaning woman we met the first night. She seemed overcome, turned quickly, and was lost in the crowd. She gave us some cassette tapes of children singing at her church and some gospel choruses she had taped from the radio to play at our Sunday school. Although our custom won't allow us to use them, she knows we appreciate her love.

Oba: The foyer and sidewalks were lined with spectators, while TV crews waited nearby. I decided the best way was to walk briskly, be polite but say nothing. Soon we were in the van and on our way.

Helen Smith wanted us to stop by the Department of Revenue Building to pick up some tax forms. Employees lined the stairs and foyer, and there were more TV cameras. Samuel, in his wheelchair, looked bewildered.

Then the seventy-mile drive to our home. We had left in panic on a hot morning in August. Now we were back on a crisp day in October. In fifty-four days, we had lived a lifetime.

My brother Monroe had placed a big sign by the road — "Welcome Home, Samuel." And another one at our house said, "Welcome Samuel, Mom, and Dad." We had a good evening, except for a bit of anxiety over the portable phone, which didn't work.

Lorene: Pat Yoder from Lincolnland Visiting Nurse Association was waiting for us at home, along with our children, daughter-in-law, and new granddaughter. Seventeen of us, not counting Pat. She changed Samuel's chest and leg bandages, and I started the first IV. Rosanna, Sue, and Rose put Samuel's things away.

Tomorrow, Paul and Rosanna will move back to their home. They've carried a big load for such a young couple with a new baby. I'll get to keep two-month-old Marneta while they move. It'll be my first time to spoil her!

For now, we put Samuel on Sue's bed and I slept with him, or at least tried to sleep. Oba slept on the couch in Sue's room. This was one of the few nights in eight weeks that Oba and I had pulled off our day clothes and slept in a real bed. But had we not stayed by Samuel's side during those long nights, he might not have been here beside me tonight. He was like someone holding on to a narrow ledge, in danger of falling into a bottomless hole. But we were there to cheer him, and he bravely held on.

Since I had the 10:00 p.m. and midnight IVs to do, I was almost afraid to go to sleep. Finally, after midnight, I relaxed, as a mother can do only when she's home and all her children are safe inside.

The storm was over. Later, we'd pick up the pieces. . . .

Part 2: The Aftermath

(Oba and Lorene as one voice)

7. Settling in for the Winter

Friends and well-wishers who followed Samuel's hospital stay have wondered how we fared when he came home. We wish we could say he went merrily on his way to school several days later, needed only an occasional aspirin for pain, that every bill was paid, and that we lived happily ever after. But life is not that simple. We have faced set-backs and victories, late-night medical crises and daytime joys, disappointments and surprise blessings.

On the positive side, six days after we returned home the administrators announced that the hospital would settle for the flat amount suggested by Helen Smith, paid entirely by the First National Bank "Friends of Samuel Herschberger" fund. We can't describe our relief nor our gratitude to so many donors and sponsors of benefits.

More good news came a week later when a number of Samuel's doctors announced that they would forego some of their fees. Nonetheless, that wasn't the end of our medical bills. Estimates of final costs including more reconstructive surgery ran to $500,000.

For example, when we came home, a portion of one bone in Samuel's leg still had no skin or flesh, and a six-day supply of IV antibiotics alone cost $2,000! Add to that the cost of dressings, home nurses, innumerable trips to Springfield, wheelchairs, crutches, prostheses, leg-lengthening, and three more major hospital stays. At times, we had to close our eyes to the mounting costs and pretend we were dreaming.

We could never have cared for a child in Samuel's

condition without the Lincolnland Visiting Nurse Association. We can't over-praise such organizations, which make home care practical. They came five days a week to check on infection, monitor what we were doing, and change the morning dressings.

Every six hours, we took turns attaching one end of a plastic line to the prepackaged bag of antibiotics and the other end to the big, needle-like opening in the shunt under Samuel's breastbone. We also helped with physical therapy and did the night dressings.

We have accepted the inevitable: Samuel faces a lifetime of problems. Hopefully, as the years go by, his problems will lessen. But the good news is that he lived! The little Amish boy who refused to die, who once told us, with quivering lips, that whenever he went to surgery he just tried to lie quietly and not cause any trouble for the doctors.

Samuel's courage through all of this has been remarkable. We know that God has been with him and with us, giving us the strength to meet the new challenges of each day. Oba also thinks that some of Samuel's toughness comes from his grandfather. When Oba was a young boy working in a furniture shop with his father, he watched as his father accidentally cut off a finger. Oba said his father stuck his hand in a bucket of turpentine, wrapped it tightly in cloth, and went back to work.

One of the first things Oba did when we were back home was to put a shield on the tractor PTO. A clerk at the store told him that many shields had been sold that fall, after news of our tragedy spread. All the time we were at the hospital, we had forbidden the children to use the PTO.

One of the nicest things about home was being surrounded by people. We didn't count all the visitors the first Sunday, but the house was full. And all afternoon, people kept coming and going. Best of all, Samuel's grandparents, Chris and Amelia Herschberger, both in their mid-eighties, arrived in a buggy from their home twelve miles away.

Nothing — not money, hospitals, doctors, cars — can replace your family. The warmth, the closeness, the security is beyond description. We sometimes feel like one big family, spread all over Moultrie and Douglas counties.

Although Samuel wasn't able to go to school that term, John Edward Schrock and Marvin Chupp brought his homework daily. Marvin, who teaches grades 1-4 in our two-room parochial school, was so overwhelmed by Samuel's condition on his first visit to the hospital that he fainted. John Edward teaches grades 5-8.

Both of these young teachers are single, and they often stayed for the evening meal, especially if Lorene served a "haystack" supper — sort of an Amish taco salad. On your plate, you form a "stack" of whatever is served you, starting with a base of rice, then adding vegetables, chopped meat, shredded cheese, tomato slices, mayonnaise, etc.

Our anxiety grew with delay after delay as we waited for permission for a permanent phone. The cellular phone seldom worked — apparently we were in the middle of two calling zones where reception was poor. One night Oba had to run to a neighbor's house to call one of the doctors. And late in another night, Pat Yoder drove out to deliver a message from a doctor who couldn't reach us. We couldn't understand the delay but had to live with it.

Finally, on November 7, three weeks after we were home, a telephone installer came. Although the doctors wanted the telephone at our bedside, we had prepared a little shack for it out in the yard. Since it was mainly for outgoing calls, this met our needs without infringing too much on our customs. A ringing phone at mealtime is something we can live without. This seems strange to others, but it pleases us. It was dark when the installer finished, so we invited him to stay for supper, which he did. It was also our twenty-third wedding anniversary.

With Samuel's bed and paraphernalia in the living room, space was a constant problem. Even before his injury, we had planned to add some rooms. But that had been delayed, and so we coped through that winter with our drafty, crowded, 108-year-old farmhouse.

Despite all the help we received, the fall of 1991 had drained us financially. Endless trips to Springfield, medications, dressings, toll call after toll call — it all mounted up. The winter of 1991-1992 pushed us to our limits.

We could afford nothing but basics, and our supply of children's clothing was low. We had added a propane wall heater to supplement our wood-burning stove, but we still shivered. Indoors we sometimes kept on our heavy coats and boots. We worried constantly that Samuel might get pneumonia or the flu.

Saturday, November 2, was bitter cold, and at 3:00 a.m. the wall heater gave out. All of us were cold, but our chief concern was Samuel. Lorene called her sister, Anna Bontrager, whose snug house in Arthur has a gas furnace, and she told us to bundle up Samuel and come to town. But that was only temporary. We couldn't move his bed and dressings and IVs to Anna's.

We were desperate, so Oba called Helen Smith, our old standby in Springfield. She came that afternoon and said the people who donated money would want some of it used for our everyday needs, as well as Samuel's medical bills. Contributions had continued to come in even after we settled our bills with the hospital and doctors. So Helen, who helped to administer the bank fund, took us to nearby Mattoon on a buying spree. We bought clothing we needed but could never afford to buy all at one time warm underwear, heavy socks, hooded sweatshirts, and boots for everyone. We also bought not one but two space heaters.

That same Sunday, in spite of all the stress on our family, our son David, sixteen, took the first step in joining the church. After a series of classes with our ministers, he will be baptized by pouring, the cup spilling over his head three times, in the name of the Father, Son, and Holy Spirit. This made the day complete — God had blessed us both materially and spiritually with manna from heaven and manna from earth. We had been concerned ever since the accident that we were neglecting the other children. But God had not forgotten David, and David had not forgotten God.

Most Amish youth profess their faith between ages sixteen and twenty. We insist they decide for themselves. Lorene started immediately to sew a mutza for David — a coat with a split tail and a narrow, stiff collar which stands up. It's the proper Sunday coat for males once they join the church.

To transport Samuel, we took one of our buggies to Willis Plank & Sons, where they cut a rear entrance with hinged doors so we could load his wheelchair and set it in the middle of two facing seats.

Eventually he was able to ride the bicycle we brought home from the hospital. After he outgrew it, we replaced it with a custom-made one, including a brake he could operate with his knee. We also made an aluminum cart to hook on the back, so he could do small errands. Even though doctors saved Samuel's right arm, he never regained more than 10 percent of his strength in it.

Another example of the human kindness we experienced came from Nancy Prill, a newspaper columnist in LaSalle, Illinois, who wrote some pieces about Samuel. She was the first to suggest that we get a battery-operated typewriter, making it easier for Samuel to write with only one hand, even with one finger. It expanded his ability to communicate and helped his attitude.

As the winter wore on, we settled into a more regular pattern of living. Although no day is "typical," we chose one entry from Lorene's journal to reprint. It's dated Saturday, November 30, 1991:

> *Last night about 11:30 we had a high wind. The older boys, who sleep in a trailer back of the house, came inside. Then the weather turned real cold. Son Paul called and wanted me to come help, as the baby's sick. So after breakfast, I went up. Showed Rosanna how to make a croup tent out of plastic to hold the steam. Little Marneta seemed to like it. Then I helped with the wash.*
>
> *There was a work frolic at David Kaufman's, so Chris went there to help. David and Joe helped Levi and Edna Herschberger repair their hog feeding floor, which blew down last night. Two of the boys stayed home to patch the shingles that blew off our hog house. I guess I should have had more boys! I always say they should be twins.*
>
> *This afternoon, took the school children to Sullivan to buy gifts for their Christmas program. Sue had a group of her friends here tonight. Steven Otto and John Mast stayed overnight, after going hunting with Chris. While they entertained each other, Oba and I went to William Otto's to visit. Between all this, Oba and I managed the IVs and a change of dressings.*

On one of our medical trips to Springfield, Governor Jim Edgar sent word he would like to meet Samuel at the Springfield headquarters of the State Police. John, William, and Philip went along too. While waiting for the Governor to arrive, Oba told the boys to smile and shake hands with this important man, look him in the eyes, and not to act nervous. He then asked them to take off their straw hats, which he held for them.

After a cordial visit, the Governor left and Oba looked at the boys' hats. In his own nervousness, he had crushed them!

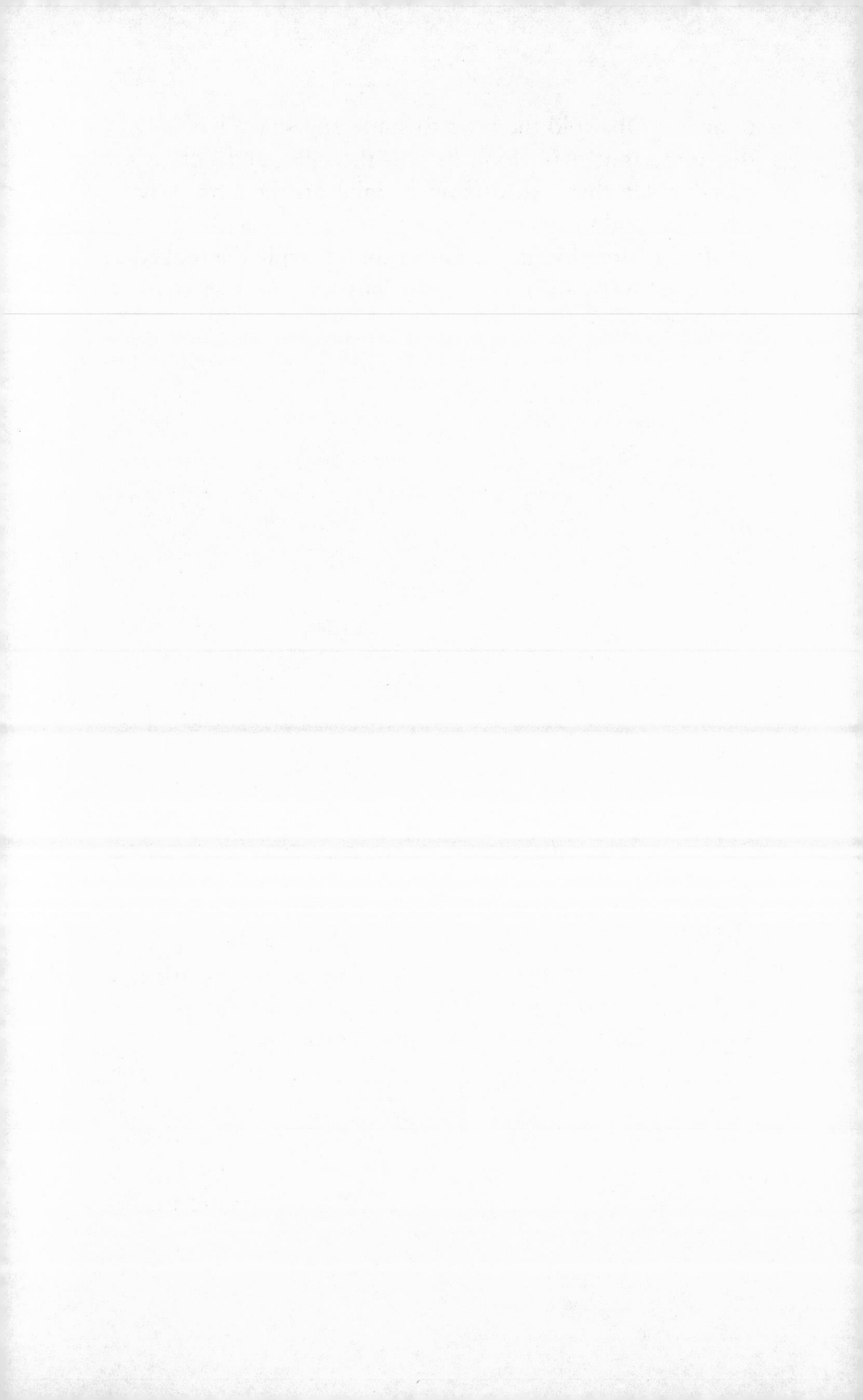

8. A Gnawing Question

For the last ten weeks of 1991, it seemed we would wear out the highway going back and forth to Springfield for checkups, two more reconstructive surgeries, and a fitting for a prosthesis.

Since we knew so many people at Memorial Hospital, it was like visiting relatives. Lorene frequently took baked goods as gifts, or to display in the staff lounge on the second floor, where they quickly sold out as the news spread by word of mouth.

One thing we never got used to was strangers coming up to us and offering to pay for our meals. Our distinctive dress made us stand out, and many of them had read Judy Miller's articles in the *State Journal-Register*. We came to sense that these donors were sincere, and that it would be rude to refuse.

In fact, the manager of the Hardee's near the hospital served us and our children free meals whenever we were in Springfield to see Samuel's doctors. It got to where he sat us at a special table; he said he was a father of three and felt for us. Lorene tried to return his graciousness by surprising him on his fiftieth birthday with a homemade black raspberry pie, the fruit picked from her own vines.

On one of our trips to Memorial, we delivered a plaque that Nelson Herschberger, Oba's second cousin, had cut from solid oak. Oba's niece, Clara Mae Yoder, lettered it and painted a cluster of flowers in one corner. We hung it outside Room 6, ICU West, seventh floor, where we'd spent so many anxious days and nights:

God, grant me the serenity
To accept the things I cannot change;
The courage to change the things I can;
And the wisdom to know the difference.
— The Samuel Herschberger Family

God bless you in your work at ICU West

We knew that eventually we must decide about Samuel's right leg, which had been shortened four inches when reattached. A temporary solution was a built-up shoe, which we got for him at Yoder's Shoe Shop south of Arthur.

As the doctors explained, we had three options:

• Amputation, then a prosthesis, which to us was out of the question.

• Stopping the growth of his left leg by surgery so that the right one could catch up with it. However, once growth was stopped on the left leg, it could not be started again. This would make him a lifetime "shorty," with legs disproportionate to his torso.

• Attempt to lengthen the bones in his right leg, in a couple of years.

Although we had doubts, number three seemed best. As we had heard briefly while Samuel was still in the hospital, a Russian doctor working in primitive conditions in Siberia had, in 1951, invented a device to lengthen or straighten bones damaged by accidents or genetics. He was Gavrijl Ilizarov, who won the 1978 Lenin Prize for Medicine. His invention, called the Ilizarov External Fixator, was discovered by the western world in 1981 and introduced at the Southern Illinois University School of Medicine in Springfield in 1989, with surgery that benefitted Devin Vannoy, as mentioned earlier.

From the start, Lorene favored the device, while Oba had reservations.

On November 25, 1991, we made the first of five trips to Shriners Hospital for Crippled Children in St. Louis. These people were extremely nice, providing us with housing and meals, and they later fitted Samuel with a new prosthesis when he outgrew his first one.

We wanted the opinions of the St. Louis doctors about the Ilizarov device, but they didn't agree among themselves. One warned that if infection set in, Samuel could die. Another felt that his leg lacked enough healthy bone and tissue for the fixator to work properly. They also showed us a slide presentation of an actual procedure. This was a mistake. It was too gory, and it frightened Samuel so much that he threw up in the van coming home. Fortunately, we had two years to decide.

Since we'd never been to St. Louis, our friend and driver Larry Neuman took us to Lambert Field to see the big jets up close — a first for us, as most Amish don't fly except for a family emergency. For some never-determined reason, Lorene didn't pass security at the airport. Who knows — maybe she was carrying one of the boy's hunting rifles under her long skirt. A more likely cause was a metal hair pin under her bonnet.

9. True Friends Never Quit

Nancy Vannoy, Devin's mother, had warned us about the risks of publicity which we could not control. Her prediction came true. Here and there, we began to sense a certain uneasiness (even among some of our fellow Amish) about the attention heaped on Samuel and the donations for his medical expenses. These feelings were not always spoken, but at times we could see envy etched in their faces.

The hardest blow came when someone reported to the Department of Children and Family Services that we were the cause of Samuel's accident, making a nine-year-old work in a dangerous environment. The social worker apologized, saying by law the agency was required to investigate, but that she was confident we were not abusive.

Yes, there's danger in working on a farm, just as there's danger in walking to school in Chicago or any other urban center.

When we hear about "deadbeat dads" who abandon their offspring and parents who let their children go hungry while they gamble and drink, we can't believe someone turned us in. However, the hundreds of well-wishers who continued to stand by us long after we came home, far outnumbered our critics. We'll never lose faith in people as a whole.

We also discovered that common tragedy sometimes brings people together. For example, soon after we came home, William and Marilyn Wood drove out from Sullivan just to talk. Their van is equipped with a lift, as they care for an adult son, Jeff, who has multiple sclerosis. They offered us rides anytime we needed them. Our hearts go out to them because of their son's crippling illness. Only as we go through dark periods ourselves can we truly sympathize with others.

A former neighbor from whom we once rented ground also came to share. He knows sorrow, for he lost a son. He told us not to blame ourselves. He used to have nightmares in which he saw his boy taking that last step into death. Then, in a dream he saw a man who looked like Jesus might have looked. Jesus was holding his son and told him not to worry, that he'd take care of the boy. After that, the nightmares ended.

One rainy December afternoon, a car pulled up and the driver gave Oba an envelope before immediately driving off. He didn't say who he was, but inside the envelope was a greeting, "The light shines in the darkness, and the darkness has not overcome it, (John 1:5)" and a handwritten note : "We lost our 34-year-old son, leaving his wife and three little girls. The love and generosity shown us was overwhelming. So please accept this as our way of saying thanks for all that was done for us." It was signed Wayne and LaVerne, but we never knew their last names. Inside with the note were ten $100 bills — a thousand dollars in cash, and it couldn't have come at a time when it was more needed.

Moral support often meant as much as money. We remember several examples:

Soon after the newspapers reported Samuel's injuries, he started getting letters every week or so from John R. Hester of Winchester, Illinois, a man we've never met. These letters were often humorous, always upbeat, and Samuel looked forward to receiving them.

Robert L. Hardin, a retired teacher in Champaign, wrote a letter we all treasure, describing a youth he had known who had overcome handicaps. He cautioned Samuel about asking questions no one can answer, such as "Why me?"

Phil Kaufman, a truck driver from Prairie Farms who picked up milk three times a week from our cooling tank, came inside one day to tell how he had lost one of his arms when he was six years old. He removed his prosthesis and explained to Samuel how it worked. He gave Samuel what he needed most at that time, which was hope.

One winter day, Irvin Thompson of Tuscola pulled up in front of our house with a pick-up-load of red wagons. He gave two of them to our children. Remembering how special a little red wagon was to him as a boy, he was going through the countryside, giving away a truckload!

John Jones from rural Arcola, who drove us on many trips in his van, told us we should write Samuel's story so others could read it. Good-naturedly, he threatened to call us once a week until we did so.

Sue Masten of Springfield, who read about us, made many trips to our home, running errands, driving us here and there.

Dr. Russell, like so many of the medical personnel, took more than a professional interest in us. He's met other Amish families and placed orders with a number of artisans, so that his office at the S.I.U. School of Medicine is now furnished with Amish-made chairs, bookcases, and desks. A nearby conference room has a large table and shelves made by local craftsmen. The same is true of shelves and cabinets in the staff kitchen.

We felt so close to the hospital personnel that we grieved when Delores Gallo, one of Samuel's favorite nurses, was stabbed one night in December of 1992. It happened in the parking lot of the hospital when someone tried to rob her. We visited her in the hospital.

Bill Keep, a chaplain in Memorial's Department of Psychiatry, had seen us from a distance while Samuel was hospitalized, but we didn't meet until months later at a funeral in our community. Our friendship with the Keeps deepened after we hosted them for a meal. From the very start they seemed at home with us. The Keeps have since moved to our area, changed their faith, and joined the Arthur Mennonite Church. Bill commutes to the hospital in Springfield, and we are close friends. He often drives out of his way to give us a ride to see Samuel's doctors.

One more example of rural friendship: One afternoon during a January blizzard, Lela Otto called, worried about the children, who were late getting home from school. She wondered if we should call the sheriff.

Oba and I hitched a buggy and started the four and a half miles to the school through blinding snow. It was zero visibility, and once we veered off the road into a field. When we reached the school, no one was there. In the storm, we had passed our own children without seeing them!

Later, we learned that one of the teachers rode home with each of the children, while the other teacher stayed at the school. Neither teacher went home until every child was safe and accounted for. A trivial incident? You be the judge.

Shortly after we returned home in the fall of 1991, the Amish community held a large auction-benefit at the pallet shop of William Otto, six miles northeast of Sullivan. It started with a pancake breakfast, then two auction rings ran for most of the day. All kinds of donated items were sold. We were pleased to learn that Dr. David Olysav, one of Samuel's surgeons, came from Springfield and bought three handmade quilts.

We were not allowed to attend the auction, because Amish custom forbids it. The reasoning is that we don't want to influence anyone to buy. Our people support benefits on the basis of the need itself, not on the personality of the one in need.

A few Saturdays later, employees of the First National Bank in Springfield held an auction in the bank's lobby — Amish chests, tables, cabinets, and chairs. A number of smaller fund-raisers were held that we knew nothing about until after the fact.

Best of all, many friends we made in the hospital have since visited our farm. Nancy Vannoy's family attended a couple of weddings. Duane took them for pony and stagecoach rides and ice skating on the farm pond. Nancy and Lorene have picked cherries together and also canned pumpkin and beets.

Our first Christmas after the accident, Larry and Donna Neuman, who had already done so much, invited us to their home for dinner on December 28. Christmas lasts longer for the Amish, for we note "Old Christmas" on January 6, as well as the traditional day on December 25.

We had eaten with non-Amish before, but not on such a festive occasion as this. There were seventeen of us, including Paul, Rosanna, and Marneta, plus ten of the Neumans, counting their children and grandchildren. Our two families melded.

Of course, we received a tremendous amount of support from within the Amish community as well as from outside. Lorene's journal is crammed with names of relatives and church people who crisscrossed our lives almost daily.

Soon after Samuel came home, Lorene resumed her turn caring for Oba's parents, Chris (whom we call Doddy, which is German for Grandpa) and Amelia (whom we call Mommy). They live in a "Grandpa" house at their old homeplace, a mile south of Arthur. A porch joins their house to the home of Lewis and Viola Schrock, their daughter and son-in-law. When he retired, Doddy built himself a "tinkering shop" to repair buggies and make wagon tongues.

Mommy had a stroke in 1989. Nearly every day since,

one of the daughters or daughters-in-law takes dinner, cleans the house, and bathes her. Lorene's turn comes about every ten days.

We are not aware of any Amish person being in a nursing home. In the final stages of Alzheimer's disease or the like, such might be necessary. But as long as we can, we look after our elderly. We never tell old people they're in the way. We revere them.

Lorene's own mother died in 1984, when her buggy was struck by a high-speed freight train at a crossing; her father died two years later.

10. We Build a House

All the time that Samuel was hospitalized, we worried about coming home to a dilapidated farmhouse. It was cold, drafty, the foundations sagging, the floors rotting. Our first thought, driven by our economic plight, was to remodel.

Help came from an unexpected source — Mary Bulpitt, the member of the Springfield Precious Moments Club who had earlier visited Samuel with a gift of $100 from the club. Shortly thereafter, she had visited the Precious Moments Chapel and headquarters near Carthage, Missouri, and had asked to meet Terri Heckmaster, personal secretary to founder Sam Butcher. Terri promised her ten minutes but listened for nearly an hour as Mary described Samuel's situation and our housing problem.

At the end of the hour, Mary said Terri was in tears and agreed to relay the story to Mr. Butcher, an artist and creator of Precious Moments giftware. With the fruits of his business success, Sam Butcher had designed and built a glorious chapel that routinely attracts up to three thousand visitors a day. It features fifty stained glass windows based on Bible stories; a fourteen-hundred-square-foot painted ceiling with an angel theme; and another painting, called the Hallelujah Square painting, picturing Jesus surrounded by nineteen children.

After being told of our situation, Mr. Butcher created a commemorative button, featuring a sketch of a small Amish farmboy wearing a broad-brimmed hat, to be used as a fundraiser. We were surprised and found it difficult to accept his generosity.

The buttons soon went on sale in all the Hallmark stores in Springfield and Charleston, at the Memorial Medical Center gift shop, and by direct mail. At first, despite our immense gratitude, we put little hope in the "button project," as we called it. But we were wrong. Thousands of buttons were sold for $1.25 each, eventually netting $20,000 for us. That was, indeed, a precious moment.

By then we had decided that building a new house made more sense than trying to salvage an old one, and so on May 29, 1992, we dug the basement and started on water lines. To our surprise and delight, workers uncovered an old well and a cistern, still in good shape. Lorene had dreamed of a cistern for soft water, and here was one ready-made. "Praise the Lord!" she cried.

With lots of volunteer help to assist the paid craftsmen, we finished the roof three weeks later and moved in. The $20,000 from Precious Moments helped a lot, but we also borrowed $40,000 and used some other resources.

Like any project that uses volunteers, we had the usual problems and delays. A year later, we were still doing odds and ends.

Today we enjoy a two-story and basement house with a big wood-burning, furnace-like stove in the basement, vented so the heat rises to the top floors. Like any Amish home, it's plain in design. There are five bedrooms and a bath upstairs and a kitchen, L-shaped living room, bedroom, and one bath downstairs. The house is not wired, since our lamps and appliances burn propane. We use no carpeting or window curtains.

The day we began digging the basement for the new house should have been a glorious day for us, but a new, heart-wrenching problem arose to cast a pale over it. One of our grown sons, who had found it difficult to cope with all that had transpired, decided to leave home. This hurt us deeply, for Amish parents pray their children will keep the faith, and when one of them doesn't, we feel responsible. In fact, one insensitive party told us that this was, indeed, our fault for focusing so much on Samuel instead of on the entire family.

We'll say no more about this situation, because the outcome is still uncertain. We console ourselves, knowing that we give our children wings as well as roots. The final decision is theirs. But it still hurts when they forsake their roots.

As soon as our new house was livable, we hosted the Jonathan Creek Church on Sunday morning, June 26, 1992. As is our custom, the entire congregation stayed for the noon meal. That's not as big a chore as it may sound like, since, by custom, it's more like a snack or picnic. The big job is the Saturday before — cleaning and storing our furniture to make room for the benches, which are brought in for the service. On Sunday nights, the "youngies" (unmarrieds age sixteen and over) meet for singing and socializing; this is a chance for a young male to try out his courting buggy.

It pleased us to host our church just days after we moved in, because these people did so much for our children while we stayed with Samuel. They were always bringing food, running errands, plus helping with the fall harvest, canning, and freezing.

Less than a year later, our farm was the setting for the marriage of our daughter Susanna to Clarence Otto. About three weeks prior, Clarence and Susanna had announced their intentions at church. Then they took buggy rides through the countryside, inviting their friends. We so wanted this to be special for Susanna, since she bore so much responsibility as the family's seventeen-year-old "mother" while we were with Samuel in Springfield.

Preparing for our daughter's wedding was a big job. The actual service would be held in our big implement shed, because we needed the house to serve the wedding dinner to our 280 guests, plus the wedding supper for about two hundred. That meant storing the furniture, setting up tables and chairs, and renting a refrigerated truck to store pies and salads. And the food: baking sixty pecan, peanut butter, and raisin cream pies, as well as thirty loaves of homemade bread; cooking forty pounds of noodles and thirty quarts of green beans; peeling seventy-five pounds of potatoes; buying sixty pounds of ham and fifty-five pounds of beef; preparing fifty quarts of Oreo pudding ice cream; plus twenty-four loaf cakes and a huge wedding cake.

The two-and-a-half-hour ceremony, which instructs the couple on the sanctity of marriage and parenthood, began at 9:00 a.m. An Amish wedding has no bridal bouquet, no rings, no honeymoon, no trousseaus, no soloists, and no photos. The bridal party wears new clothing, but it's Sunday wear, not formal. Wedding gifts are often wrapped within a gift, say cookware wrapped in a bath towel. This saves on giftwrap, which is usually tossed anyway.

After the sit-down dinner, the bride receives guests in an upstairs bedroom, where all the gifts are displayed. A personal thank-you takes the place of notes. If this seems odd, remember that Amish brides spend an entire afternoon visiting with the guests, rather than posing for photographs and hurrying off to honeymoons.

A wedding supper follows the evening chores. The adults then gradually leave, and the young people sing until bedtime. By 11:00 p.m., the long line of buggies parked near the barn in neat rows were gone.

It was a wonderful day, and we were doubly pleased when one of Samuel's surgeons, Dr. Russell, and his wife, Anne, attended. Since he reads German and knew some

Amish people while growing up in Millersburg, Ohio, he could follow the ceremony. Our worlds continued to criss-cross.

11. The Most Dreaded Surgery

Samuel continued to be in and out of the hospital so often that some of his ordeals are blurred in our minds. But three of them we will always remember distinctly.

When Samuel's torn scalp was reattached, half of it died, in spite of heroic efforts to save it. So in February of 1992, his doctors lifted the good half of his scalp and inserted two "balloons," made of expandable silicone, under it. For weeks, we injected saline water into the balloons, gradually expanding them. As the balloons swelled, they stretched the skin, multiplying the portion of hair-growing scalp.

It was an amazing procedure, and it worked! After about three months, the surgeons reaped nearly enough good skin and hair to cover the half of his scalp that had died.

Most patients return to the hospital, say, once a week, for more saline water. But Lorene thought she could do it herself, saving the time and expense of hospital visits. Moreover, by injecting water daily (rather than weekly), the growth was hastened.

Unfortunately, Samuel suffered a severe reaction two days after the implant. His head began swelling and he had muscle spasms, arching his back and head. He was in terrible pain, and one time he screamed, "Jesus, let me die!" The crisis lasted a day and a half.

Fearing the worst, we sent for all the children. Word quickly spread at home, and John Mast called from Arcola, asking if it was true that Samuel had died. Oba Helmuth, the coffin maker, also wondered if he should start on a casket. (Our custom is that the church buys the materials, then

Oba custom-makes each coffin to fit the deceased.)

Fortunately, the crisis passed. And there was no problem when a similar expander (to grow skin for raw places on one of Samuel's legs) was later implanted on the right side of his back.

The question that dogged us, however, was whether to try the Ilizarov Fixator on his shortened, right leg. At one point, Lorene said it was too much to decide on our own; she longed for the advice of her parents, both deceased. She had some bad dreams and wrote in her journal about a lump in her throat that wouldn't go away, like when her parents died.

We accepted an invitation from Nancy Vannoy to visit the North Medical Center in Minneapolis, where her son Devin was still seeing Dr. Van Beek for check-ups. We left Springfield on Wednesday, February 24, 1993, in Nancy's aging diesel station wagon. It was a bitterly cold day, and engine problems in Clinton delayed us. Lorene stuffed a pillow between us and the door, where the cold air was coming in.

It was fourteen degrees below zero when we reached the farm home of Oba's brother, Chris, near Wautoma, Wisconsin. We sat up until 4:45 a.m., visiting. Thursday morning, almost sleepless from the night before, we headed on to Minneapolis. By then the temperature had dropped to thirty degrees below zero!

Dr. Van Beek looked at Samuel's X rays and agreed with Drs. Russell and Olysav about the fixator: "If he were my boy, I'd do it." That settled it. The long months of indecision were over.

It was too late to drive back to Springfield, so we stayed with Amish friends, Ernest and Wilma Graber and their son Joseph, eighteen, near Hillsboro, Wisconsin. We almost didn't find their house. Stopped four times for directions. We drove and drove with snow and ice everywhere. At one point, when we dead-ended into a snowbank, Devin jumped out in the dark and gave a big war whoop. At least we had fun!

Oba sat up a long time talking with Ernest, and since we left at 4:00 a.m., he, again, got little sleep. But to the Amish, nothing's better than visiting with your friends. Three months later we learned that Joseph was tragically killed in a logging accident.

The following September, Dr. Gordon Allan placed the Ilizarov Fixator on Samuel's right leg. Although we had agonized for months and the morning newspaper headline warned, "Amish Boy Faces 23rd, and Most Feared, Operation," it went smoothly.

After Samuel was home, we gave each of the thirteen pins in the device a half-millimeter turn, four times a day. These thirteen pins, inserted in his ankle and leg bones, were held in place by two, halo-like metal cylinders. Tightening the pins created tension, causing the bones to expand and grow.

Called the "orthopedic discovery of the century," it slowly did what the doctors had predicted. Modern technology, so foreign to many of our Amish ways, was giving a young boy (and his parents) greater hope for his future.

12. Our Twenty-fifth Anniversary

Just six days after Samuel's fixator surgery, Lorene broke her leg, putting two members of the family in wheelchairs at the same time. Lorene's injury was a good deal less dramatic (and more embarrassing) than Samuel's surgery — she broke it while jumping on the kids' trampoline.

The children bought the trampoline with money they had earned cutting weeds from the neighbor's soybeans. Mary Anna, our five-year-old, had begged Lorene to show her how to jump.

We noted our twenty-fifth wedding anniversary on Sunday, November 7, 1993. Nothing formal, just talking with neighbors and friends who had come to visit Lorene while she was recuperating.

On anniversaries people tend to reminisce about all that's happened, both good and bad. We've had lots of good, including thirteen lively children with no serious health problems, until Samuel's accident. But on this anniversary, the trauma of the past two years dominated our memories. An ordeal like this tends to overshadow everything else, and it brings on emotional as well as physical stress. At times, we bordered on nervous or emotional breakdowns. Two factors helped see us through. First, occasional medication. Second, and most important, friends we could turn to who would listen when we needed to talk.

Still, Oba found it difficult to sleep longer than six hours at a time without waking, questioning, and wondering about the future.

Both of us, as well as our older children, ended our

schooling with the eighth grade, as is customary for Amish children. When Samuel finishes, we don't know what he'll be able to do. The State Department of Rehabilitation has offered help with job training, and although we've had no big success in selling, we've become Amway distributors, thinking this is something Samuel might be able to pursue. We do know he'll never be able to do vigorous farm work.

Although doctors saved Samuel's right arm, the muscles are so weak that he has to make a fist to clutch a pen, even to write. His right hand is so weak he must prop one finger on top of another to push down a single key of his battery-powered typewriter. Although one leg is still several inches shorter than the other, and both legs are turned in, Samuel walks without assistance.

Even after thirty-four operations, his future holds many unknowns. However, he's alive — the Amish farm boy whom doctors said shouldn't live, given his injuries.

More than ever we appreciate the role of education, for without advanced training, Samuel's doctors and nurses would have been helpless to care for him. Without a speeding ambulance, he likely would have died enroute to the hospital. We acknowledge and give thanks for those facets of modernity, but in our culture, togetherness is valued more than technology.

We often think about Samuel's future — his medical needs, his lifework. But we have faith that there will be a way. He never complains. He's quiet, thoughtful, and enjoys sitting and listening to the older men talk. Since he doesn't complain, why should we? We sometimes think a handicap is harder for the parents to accept than the youngster.

One winter day, Samuel was sitting by the window, watching the children play in the snow. Tears rolled down his cheeks. Lorene put her arms around him and held him.

No words were needed.

At first, Memorial Medical Center offered to arrange for a child psychiatrist, but it was decided Samuel didn't need therapy. He's gotten to where he can even laugh about his injuries. At mealtime, when we ask the children to fold their hands in prayer, he will clap his only hand to the opposite shoulder and laugh.

In the fall of 1995, we were hosting the Keep and Vannoy families for a meal. We got to talking about how we had formed so many non-Amish friendships during our ordeal, and we wondered what we could do to strengthen those ties and to show our appreciation to the "outside" world.

We decided to open our home on Friday and Saturday nights to the general public, to offer them the opportunity to come and share a real Amish meal. Well, the idea succeeded far beyond our dreams. We now serve up to sixty guests each of those nights, and we are booked with reservations months in advance.

We serve a typical Amish meal, family style, such as home-baked bread and jams, ham or meatloaf, mashed potatoes and gravy, homemade noodles, a vegetable and salad, and always ice cream, maybe with strawberries, angel cake, or pecan pie.

We move long tables and folding chairs into our living/dining area, and the whole family pitches in to help cook, serve, and clean up. We don't have a set price for the meals, but rather we operate on a donation basis — whatever our guests want to pay. The revenue helps us meet unforeseen costs of future medical expenses and rehabilitation for Samuel.

But best of all is sitting around the tables with our guests, throwing shadows across the room from the light of our propane lamps, talking, sharing, and laughing. We Amish are strong on visiting and talking (which is why we function so well without television).

Before the evening is over, many of our guests enjoy a short buggy ride around the farm. They often explain that they wanted to meet some plain and simple people because they were curious about our way of life.

Who knows what this venture could open up in the way of careers in food service or management for some of our children, including Samuel? With increasing costs of land, it's more difficult for young Amish males to make a living on farms. This gives us concern, because our traditional, rural culture meant families stayed intact, that children grew up learning to work and do their daily chores.

We're also concerned that as our youth are exposed more and more to what we call a "worldly lifestyle," our families will be threatened.

As one of the many fundraisers for Samuel, the staff and students at Lincoln Land Community College in Springfield published *Recipes for Samuel*, a cookbook put together by Suzi Mielkaitis, Jane Rutherford, and Rhonda Bowden.

A verse in the front of the book by Helen Steiner Rice summarizes our feelings about all that's happened to our family since that fateful day in 1991:

> *People need people and friends need friends. And we all need love, for a full life depends not on vast riches or great acclaim, but just in knowing that someone cares and holds us close in their thoughts and prayers. For only the knowledge that we're understood makes everyday living feel wonderfully good.*

To correspond with the Herschbergers, please write them at:

Route 1, Box 218
Sullivan, IL 61951

ABOUT THE AUTHOR:

Robert J. Hastings began writing about family and small town life in 1972, when Southern Illinois University Press published his boyhood memoirs, *A Nickel's Worth of Skim Milk: A Boy's View of the Great Depression*. This book, which describes what it was like to grow up in the home of a jobless coal miner in Marion, Illinois, won numerous awards and is the best selling book published by the University. In 1986, SIU Press published an award-winning sequel, *A Penny's Worth of Minced Ham: Another Look at the Great Depression*. He received a graduate degree at Southwestern Baptist Theological Seminary in Ft. Worth, Texas. Some of his other books are *Tinyburg Tales, We Were There*, and *The Answer Book for Writers and Storytellers*. His short essay, "The Station," was reprinted by Reader's Digest and columnist Ann Landers. Friends of Lincoln Library named him Springfield Writer of the year (1996) for his nonfiction work, *Samuel: The Amish Boy Who Lived*, the first published version of this book. Mr. Hastings died in January, 1997.